Looking Through the Faraway End

Creating a Literature-Based Reading Curriculum With Second Graders

Lee Galda
University of Minnesota
Minneapolis, Minnesota, USA

Shane Rayburn
University of Georgia
Athens, Georgia, USA

Lisa Cross Stanzi
David C. Barrow Elementary School,
Athens, Georgia, USA

INTERNATIONAL
Reading
® **Association**

800 Barksdale Road, PO Box 8139
Newark, Delaware 19714-8139, USA
www.reading.org

The International Reading Association attempts, through its publications, to provide a forum for a wide spectrum of opinions on reading. This policy permits divergent viewpoints without implying the endorsement of the Association.

Director of Publications   Joan M. Irwin
Assistant Director of Publications   Jeanette K. Moss
Editor in Chief, Books   Matthew W. Baker
Permissions Editor   Janet S. Parrack
Associate Editor   Tori Mello
Publications Coordinator   Beth Doughty
Association Editor   David K. Roberts
Production Department Manager   Iona Sauscermen
Art Director   Boni Nash
Senior Electronic Publishing Specialist   Anette Schütz-Ruff
Electronic Publishing Specialist   Cheryl J. Strum
Electronic Publishing Assistant   Jeanine K. McGann

Project Editor   Janet S. Parrack

Cover photo   Lisa Cross Stanzi. Book shown in photo is *Bunnicula: A Rabbit Tale of Mystery* (1979) by D. & J. Howe and illustrated by Alan Daniel. New York: Simon & Shuster. Reproduced with permission.

Library of Congress Cataloging in Publication Data

Galda, Lee.
Looking through the faraway end : creating a literature-based reading curriculum with second graders / Lee Galda, Shane Rayburn, Lisa Cross Stanzi.
    p. cm. – (Kids InSight series)
Includes bibliographical references and index.
1. Reading (Primary)--United States--Case studies. 2. Second grade (Education)--United States--Case studies. 3. Curriculum planning--United States--Case studies. 4. Reading groups--United States--Case studies.
I. Rayburn, Shane. II. Stanzi, Lisa Cross. III. Title. IV. Series.
LB1525 .G26 2000
372.4--dc21   00-27789

This book is dedicated to the children
who allowed us to watch them
as they became sophisticated readers.

Thank you

· Achala, Amarachi, Brett, Cameron, Cheng, Chris,
Jasmyn, Maria, Pilar, Sarah, Shida, and Will

Special thanks to Barb Wright
for her welcome support.

Contents

Note From the Series Editor

It is a pleasure to introduce readers to Lee Galda, Shane Rayburn, Lisa Stanzi, and the wonderful young people in Lisa's second-grade classroom. The voices of Lisa's students and the story of their collaborative journey toward motivated, meaningful literacy learning is detailed in one of the first books to be published in the Kids InSight series.

The Kids InSight series provides practical information for K–12 teachers and brings to the fore the voices of, and stories about, children and adolescents as the basis for instructional decisions. Books in the series are designed to encourage educators to address the challenge of meeting the literacy needs of all students in our classrooms—as learners and individuals—while recognizing that there are no easy answers or quick fixes to achieving this goal. A sociocultural perspective of how students learn forms the foundation of each Kids InSight book, and authors address learners' emotional, affective, and cognitive development. Dialoguing with other professionals, reading research findings in literacy and education in general, inquiring into teaching and learning processes, observing as well as talking and listening to students, documenting successful practices, and reflecting on literacy events using writing and analysis are strategies and actions embraced by teachers described in the books in this series. Authors of books allow us to see into classrooms and learn about the thoughts and dreams of students as well as the goals and planning processes of teachers. Finally, we are privy to seeing how events actually unfold during formal and informal lessons—the successful and the less-than-successful moments—through the use of transcripts and interview comments woven throughout Kids InSight books.

Lee, Lisa, and Shane show us how to keep kids in sight during literature discussions. For example, we learn how listening closely to individuals, as well as groups of students, and helping them clarify their thinking via carefully timed questions, allowed Lisa to support second graders as they talked about character traits, feelings, and motives while reading high quality literature like *The Whipping Boy*. As we read transcripts of small-group interactions, we also see how Lisa gleaned important insights about learners. When a student, Pilar, offered a comment that seemed out of place during a book discussion, Lisa, who was very familiar with the book and with Pilar's knowledge and thinking strategies, provided the right question that allowed Pilar to clarify her answer and contribute to the group conversation. By following Lisa during a school year, we see how she evolved into a teacher who seems to know just when to nudge or encourage a student, and when to remain silent, pondering what is revealed in a phrase, a glance, or a written comment.

We also see how a teacher's strong knowledge base in literacy and child development supports her as she seeks to be a responsive, planful teacher. For example, Lisa shows us how her knowledge of books, children, and the literacy skills children need to develop are infused into her daily actions and interactions with students. This knowledge allows her to orchestrate rich and well-informed literature discussion in which she guides the students' conversations yet takes her cues from their questions and revelations and encourages their independence as learners.

Finally, Lee, Lisa, and Shane talk about the gift of story and time that Lisa gave to her second graders. This is also a gift the three authors give to those of us who read about the tensions one teacher and two teacher-researchers grapple with and the successes Lisa and her students experience as a result of the informed risks all individuals were willing to take to meet the literacy needs of all kids.

Deborah R. Dillon
Series Editor
Purdue University
West Lafayette, Indiana, USA

Kids InSight Review Board

Melvin L. Thursby
Prairie Middle School
Cedar Rapids, Iowa, USA

Jan Turbill
University of Wollongong
Wollongong, New South Wales,
    Australia

Angela Ward
University of Saskatchewan
Saskatoon, Saskatchewan,
    Canada

Deborah A. Wooten
Glenwood Landing School
Glen Head, New York, USA

Josephine P. Young
Arizona State University
Tempe, Arizona, USA

Chapter 1

Setting the Context

> *Over lunch one January day, Lee, a university researcher, was read-ing aloud Patricia MacLachlan's* Arthur, for the Very First Time *(1987). The second-grade literature group had asked to read the book again almost as soon as they had finished it the first time in November. Lisa, the classroom teacher, has asked Lee if she'd like to read aloud to the group, so they arrange to eat lunch in Lisa's room for a few weeks in January, eating while Lee reads. They have just listened to the chapter in which Uncle Wrisby and Arthur talk about the telescope that's in Arthur's bedroom. Uncle Wrisby remarks that Arthur might want to look through "the faraway end" sometime, and Arthur wonders why. Lee asks the children why he might want to do that, but they have little to say, and there is no time left for discussion.*
>
> *Three months later in April, the windows are open to spring. As Lee enters the classroom, Amarachi runs up, smiles, and shyly hugs her, al-most whispering, "I know why you might want to look through the far-away end." Lee, amazed, asks why, and Amarachi replies, "Well, I was looking through my binoculars at a bird in a tree. When I looked through the close-up end, I saw the bird, but when I looked through the faraway end, I saw the whole tree."*

The gift of story and time that Lisa was able to give her second-grade students allowed Amarachi the freedom to use literature to think about her life as she was learning to read. Her newly found understanding of how the way we view the world affects what we see gave us, the three adults who watched her grow as a reader, the perfect metaphor for what we had been doing during the year. Lee and Shane, university researchers, and Lisa, a teacher-researcher, had been looking closely as 12 young readers made meaning together, and we had been looking through the faraway end, seeking to understand the pattern of the literary dance that allowed them to make meaning of the texts. As we did this, we discovered the importance of balancing the close-up with the faraway, and came to see this balance as integral to the responsive teaching that Lisa did.

But, of course, it wasn't always like this. One day had been so frustrating that Lisa wrote in her journal:

> Ugh! The discussion was as drizzly as the rain. Students wanted to (again) talk about the chicken pecking! Pilar and Amarachi hadn't read the chapter. I missed Shida and Achala's voices. Why didn't they talk? Cheng and Jasmyn still don't listen in discussion. The 70 minutes dragged on. Shane and I had a good laugh (later) about the arduous discussion.

The very next day Lee wrote in her field notes: "These kids need to learn to be quiet and think before speaking!" But even bad days like those two drizzly November mornings were opportunities for change and growth, which is what we all did. This is the story of students in one second-grade reading group and their growth as readers, as literate thinkers, and as participants in conversations about books. It is also about the struggles, doubts, fears, and ultimate triumphs of Lisa, their teacher. This book is about change, as Lisa sought to transform her basal-reading curriculum into practices that looked more like a literature-study group, but without losing opportunities to teach students how to read, write, think, and discuss the books she offered them. This is also a record of a collaboration between school and university that helped to change all our understandings of what it is to be a teacher.

Reflection Point

Obtain a journal where you can record your thoughts. Think about what interests you as a teacher. Write about what you notice, what you care about, and what you wonder about. As you read this book, add to your list of wonderings. You might want to use a double-entry journal in which you write on the left-hand page, keeping the right-hand page clear for subsequent reflection and analysis.

Who Are We and Why Are We Writing This Book?

This book began with a friendship born out of shared interests in children and their books. Lisa, a student at the University of Georgia and a second-grade teacher at Barrow Elementary School in Clarke County, Georgia; Shane, a doctoral student at the University of Georgia; and Lee, then a professor at the University of Georgia, met when Lisa and Shane took courses taught by Lee. One spring day, Lisa remarked that it would be fun to work on a research project together. When school began the following fall, we embarked on a year-long study of Lisa's second-grade reading group. We began with questions about teaching reading, writing, and literature, and a methodology designed to help us answer those questions. As we observed, recorded, and discussed what the children were doing and saying, we developed more questions.

Our schedule called for Lee to observe the group on Tuesday and Thursday mornings, Shane to observe on Monday and Wednesday mornings, and both to observe on Fridays, followed by an hour discussion with Lisa about our observations, the instructional decisions Lisa was making, and plans for the following week. With few exceptions, this schedule was followed throughout the school year. We recorded our observations on laptop computers; these fieldnotes described what occurred each day and were supplemented with audiotapes and videotapes of group interactions. Lisa kept a journal. The ideas that appear in the following chapters are based on the recorded data.

However, this book is more than data. It is a product of three lives that have been intimately connected with children and books for a long time. Lee has taught for 30 years, working with students from 3 to 60 years old. Her passion for and knowledge of children and their books keeps her in classrooms, as a parent volunteer and as a researcher. She is especially interested in how children make sense of what they read, using cues from both the text and their own experiences. Shane has taught both general and special education classes in urban and suburban elementary and secondary schools. One of his passions is literature and linking life to literature both inside and outside the classroom. He wants to know how children make sense of the world around them through literature and through telling stories about their own lives. Lisa, an award-winning teacher with 10 years of experience, also passionate about children's literature, was interested in how her students were making sense of what they were reading and how they responded to the stories, poems, and nonfiction literature that surrounded them. Lisa's reading of theory and research as a graduate student informed her practice as a teacher, just as her practice informed her critique of theory and research.

What Do We Believe About Teaching and Learning?

The three of us shared these interests, and we also shared a view of teaching and learning literacy. Literacy, for us, is the practice of reading, writing, viewing, talking, and creating other symbolic representations. It involves all modes of expression including dance, drama, writing, music, and art, and rests on the social nature of talk. As children encounter opportunities for literate practices in the classroom, they make sense of these opportunities and practice the routines that are appropriate to them while in the company of others. Teaching involves being responsive to children's needs, and understanding their strengths and weaknesses (and knowing how to address them). It involves planning and being instantaneously responsive. Teaching requires a balance between taking cues from students and bringing to bear a knowledge of content, standards, requirements, and how children learn. Moving back and forth between held knowledge and knowledge in the making while observing what students are doing, reflective teachers make instructional decisions. These decisions require flexibility that is disciplined rather than random, a dynamic tension that encourages risk taking on the part of students and teachers, but within the security of a supportive group. Teaching becomes an opportunity for allowing discovery, for making things possible, and for explicit instruction, and an opportunity for renewal and growth. We hope this book will become an opportunity for renewal and growth as you read about the events in Lisa's classroom while you think about your own teaching. For us, watching the children make sense of their lives, their books, and their literate practices was an opportunity for growth and renewal that profoundly influenced our teaching and learning lives.

Who Are the Children?

Lisa's reading group that year was indeed a special group. In her school, children were grouped across classrooms for 70-minute periods of reading instruction. Lisa's group (called BRAG, or Barrow Readers Achieve Goals) consisted of five students from her class and six or seven children from another second-grade class. The remaining children in her class went to other teachers for reading instruction. This was an unusual way of grouping for reading instruction, but the school had found that smaller groups among several teachers (classroom teachers and specialists) and intense focus on reading every day were quite effective for their students. The school based its reading instruction on a basal series adopted by the county. The previous year's instruction for these students had been a combination of basal instruction enlivened and enriched by children's trade books.

Lisa's school was located across the street from a university athletic facility and served a richly diverse population. Out of an enrollment of approximately 375 prekindergarten through fifth-grade students, 55.7% were African American or multiracial, 27.5% European American, 11.2% Asian, and 5.6% Latino; and 70% of students qualified for free or reduced lunch. Further, 24% of first- through fifth-grade students were designated as gifted, and 12% were eligible for special education services. Students came from throughout the county, where there was a controlled school-choice plan in effect, and from very diverse neighborhoods, including university graduate-student family housing. There was a lengthy waiting list for placement at the school. Lisa's homeroom class consisted of 21 students—11 boys and 10 girls.

Lisa's reading group reflected the diversity that characterized the school. At the beginning of the year, there were 11 students—5 boys and

6 girls—from diverse cultural backgrounds. There was African American, Indian, European American, Asian, and multiracial representation among the group. Eight students were identified as academically gifted according to state standards. All were reading at or above grade level according to standardized tests and teacher-administered informal reading inventories. Although they were together only for a short time each day, they developed a group persona, often carrying it with them outside the classroom. One student, Chris, remarked, "In here we read differently. We think about what we read."

Chris turned 8 during fall of second grade. A voracious reader, he often veiled his emotional responses to books through humor. He was very good at imitating a character, and often delighted and entertained the group by responding with a character's voice and actions. Chris assumed a leadership role during discussions. He spent time with both his parents, who were divorced and had advanced degrees.

Maria turned 8 in the spring of second grade. Her long hair often hid her quiet smile. She was an intent listener and a thoughtful speaker. When she decided to share and respond, it was most likely an important comment or connection. She spent time after school with both her parents, who were professionals, and a new stepmother.

Amarachi, who turned 8 in December, almost always greeted those she knew with a shy smile and a hug. Initially reserved in group discussions, she only responded when called on. Then she would share without hesitation, and her responses revealed a thoughtful, reflective reader. By year end, Amarachi voluntarily shared not only her responses, but also many wonderful folktales learned from her mother. Her parents, both Nigerian, were graduate students at the university.

Cameron, who turned 7 a few weeks before school began (one of the youngest in the group) was far from shy. A free spirit with a rich and active imagination, Cameron always had a positive and encouraging manner. He never hesitated to jump into group conversations, inviting others to join him. Cameron demonstrated, by example, how to make links across books or intertextual connections. During group discussions he contributed many links to other books he had read. He had a close relationship with his mother, who was working toward a nursing degree.

Pilar made connections that were usually between her own life and the literature she was reading, which helped others remember to make these important connections. Although Pilar did not always remember to do her reading assignments and written responses, she was an important member of the group. She lived with her mother, a middle school teacher; her father, a graduate student; and an older brother.

Jasmyn loved to talk and always had something interesting to say. A born actress, she knew how to hold the attention of an audience. As the year progressed, she learned how to yield gracefully and let others have a turn in the spotlight. A very intelligent girl who made very relevant and insightful comments and connections, Jasmyn lived with her mother.

Cheng, born in China, had entered school in the United States as a kindergartener speaking no English. A small boy with a large voice, Cheng was very direct. He had a delightful sense of humor and a constant smile. Very eager to learn, he was not shy about asking the meaning of a word or for help in understanding something that had occurred in a story. His father was a graduate student. Sadly for us all, Cheng moved in December.

Achala, born in India, also left the group in late fall. Like Cheng, she came to school as a kindergartener speaking no English, but by second grade was fluently bilingual. She loved to read and devoured many books; it was not uncommon for her to read an entire chapter book in one night. She was a thoughtful, quiet student who weighed her words carefully before responding. Her father, too, was a graduate student.

Brett joined the group in November, moving to Lisa's group from another reading group. Red-haired, freckled, and with a bright, infectious smile, Brett enjoyed a good laugh. She was very involved in soccer and skiing, was enthusiastic and quite knowledgeable about dinosaurs, and was an excellent student. Although reserved when she first joined the group, she took on a leadership role and was a very active participant by the end of the year. Her father traveled a lot on business, and her mother was a school nutritionist.

Will was with the group until March. A very active student who was easily distracted, Will nevertheless tried hard to please and be a part of the group. However, he presented a challenge to smooth group dynamics by becoming impatient, sarcastic, and antagonistic to other group members. Sometimes he did not read and respond in preparation for group time or he would remain silent. When he did participate, he most often played the role of interpreter, helping his fellow classmates to understand one another. Will spent time with both parents, who were divorced.

Shida came to the United States from China when he was 4. As a kindergartner, he attended English as a second language classes and quickly became fluent in English. Shida was a serious student, and the group looked forward to his quietly delivered insights about the many books he read. He was also a gifted artist and well respected by all his classmates. His father was a graduate student.

Sarah was a gift to us all. As she would freely tell you, she would rather run and play soccer than read a book. She had great confidence in her athletic skills, but wasn't sure of herself as a reader. However, it was Sarah who consistently reminded us of the pure joy in reading. She loved beautiful words and illustrations. Although she began the year as the weakest silent reader, her oral comprehension and verbal ability was astounding. She quickly became a strong leader in the group. She lived with her mother, the assistant principal of the school, and her father, a scientist.

These children came together for 70 minutes every morning, forming a circle of readers who quickly called themselves the "literature group," and who, as Chris said, learned to think deeply and well about what they read. This book will show their learning and thinking. We do not tell any story but our own—that of a small group of good readers who spent their second-grade year together, and that of three teachers and researchers who spent a year watching them. However, even though the group configuration and the children themselves were unique, much of what happened that year could happen anywhere, with any children and teachers willing to do the kind of responsive, literature-based teaching that Lisa did. We invite you to read this book for possibilities, looking for what you might do to change your teaching and learning.

The chapters in this book are organized around questions that are often asked when we talk about our year together. Chapter 2 describes how Lisa helped her students learn to think and talk about the literature they were reading, and gives examples of instructional and emotional support that enabled them to do so. Chapter 3 describes ways in which Lisa helped her students explore ideas ranging from how stories work to differences among realism, fantasy, and nonfiction. At the same time, Lisa also helped her students develop as fluent and successful readers. Chapter 4 explores the kinds of reading strategy lessons that were embedded in the literature discussion group. Finally, Chapter 5 closes with a discussion of assessment, both the ongoing assessment at the heart of Lisa's stance as a child-centered, responsive teacher and the formal assessment that showed her students did, indeed, learn what they needed—and much, much more.

We organized our thoughts this way in order to answer the questions most frequently asked about this project, but in reality all the things Lisa did happened together. In any daily classroom interaction, you would be likely to hear Lisa helping children learn how to be good group members, how to develop their comprehension skills, and how a particular aspect of literature works. You would also see her making notes about each student's activities and constantly assessing where students are and where they need to go. Consequently, we have "revisited" conversations throughout the chapters so you can see the complexity of Lisa's teaching. Actually, as you read the stories about these young readers, you can see for yourself.

Reflection Point_____

Recall a recent segment of time in your classroom (a day, a week, a unit) and the lessons that you hoped you were teaching and your students were learning. List these lessons in terms of learning how to do things and learning about things. Keep this as a running list of the strategies and actions that you are teaching and the content of your teaching. As you continue to read, think about this list, reflecting on your strengths as a teacher, the focus of your lessons, and what might be missing from your lessons.

Discussion as a Way of Learning

As you will discover, group discussion was the primary vehicle for the teaching and learning that occurred in Lisa's classroom. Talking with students about books allowed her to accomplish the goals she had set for herself and her students. Lisa knew the importance of discussion because she had experimented with it the previous year and was amazed and delighted at the conversations her students engaged in. She had also been reading a number of books on literature instruction (Daniels, 1994; Newkirk & McClure, 1992; Samway & Whang, 1996; Short & Pierce, 1990), and knew there was a sound research base that assured that discussion was an effective way of learning from text and from each other (Gambrell & Almasi, 1996; McMahon, 1997). This, coupled with her knowledge of reader response (Langer, 1995; Rosenblatt, 1978), narrative (Bruner, 1986, 1990), and the social nature of learning (Bakhtin, 1981, 1986; Vygotsky, 1978) helped create the general framework of her literature curriculum for the year.

She discovered, for example, that small-group discussion is an effective means for engaging students in creating knowledge together or in socially constructing what they knew. Because the students were working together, they could do and understand more than they could alone. They brought their many, varied ideas to the group, and the experience of individuals in the group was richer for it. Once the group learned how to work together an important scaffolding (Vygotsky, 1978) function was served as the members supported one another in their quest for meaning.

As students learned to work together, they developed and practiced important interpersonal skills, such as how to accept others' ideas politely, even when they disagreed with them; how to listen to each other; and how to comment on each other's contribution to the discussion. They also learned to assess their own communicative ability by monitoring the responses of their peers to determine whether their own ideas had been clearly stated and understood.

Discussion, then, was at the heart of Lisa's reading program. As you read this book, listen to the voices of Lisa's students as they become increasingly sophisticated readers and conversationalists. Listen to how they learned from each other, and how we learned from them.

*Reflection Point*_____

Think about what literacy means in your classroom and in your life. Write your definition of literacy in your journal. Then over time, observe yourself and your students as you engage in literacy practices. Write down what you observe on index cards. Later, record your notes in your journal. Periodically, read and think about what you have written. How does what you do reflect what you believe? How does it not?

_____

Chapter 2

How Can I Help My Students Become Powerful Conversationalists About Books? Just Jump Right In!

The literature group is gathered in a circle, books on their laps and reading logs under the chairs. The conversation proceeds with stops and starts, and the students, uneasy and unsure, look toward Lisa for direction. Finally, Jasmyn and Cheng begin to speak, simultaneously. They hesitate, smile with some embarrassment, and stop. Cameron speaks up: "Just jump right in!" he says, reminding them of what Lisa has been saying for several weeks since school began. This reminder from a peer helps to relax the group, and they do, indeed, begin to jump right in.

The students in Lisa's class did not enter second grade knowing how to talk with each other about books. What they were asked to do in literature group was new to them and, like most things new, it took time for them to be successful. Not surprisingly, the road to success was marked by detours as well as progress. As we observed the literature group and discussed our observations, we came to realize that many kinds of lessons and learning were occurring. We also discovered that Lisa was supporting the children's attempts to discuss the books they were reading through a variety of strategies that changed over the year as the students' abilities and needs changed.

BOX 2-1
Guidelines for Asking Good Questions During Discussion-Group Sessions

1. Ask questions that are brief and clear, but don't ask too many questions. Let the students talk more than you.
2. Wait 15 seconds before asking another question. Sometimes questions require thoughtful answers; give students time to think.
3. Listen to what students say, and ask questions that encourage them to expand on what they are saying. Sometimes simply repeating their words with a rising intonation is enough.
4. Ask questions that require students to infer, predict, hypothesize, and evaluate as well as questions that require them to recall, define, and compare or contrast.
5. Ask questions that permit students to question their own ideas and assumptions, which helps them become aware of their logic.
6. Ask open-ended questions, which allow for a variety of answers. Open-ended questions have no one right answer. Accept a variety of answers and encourage several students to respond.
7. Give students the opportunity to ask questions—of you and of each other. Before they came to school, students learned a great deal about their world by asking questions. Allow them to continue to learn in this manner.

From Galda, L., Cullinan, B.E., & Strickland, D.S. (1979). *Language, literacy, and the child* (2nd ed.). New York: Harcourt Brace.

First, Lisa and the children had to learn to listen. Lisa had to develop her skills as an attentive and responsive listener, and the children had to learn to listen to each other and think about what they heard. Second, Lisa spent time in the beginning of the year setting tasks and procedures that supported the children in their conversations. Third, Lisa taught her students to monitor themselves as readers and thinkers, as well as group members. Fourth, Lisa demonstrated how the children could use their journal entries as a springboard for discussion, offering prompts and asking questions that encouraged them to respond aesthetically when they were reading stories and poems (see Box 2-1). Fifth, and perhaps most important, Lisa was quite deliberate in her selection of books the children were reading and responding to.

Learning to Listen

Really listening to children is one of the most important and rewarding skills in a teacher's repertoire. Listening to children is an essential part of being a responsive teacher because it allows us to find out what they know, how they think, what they are confused about, and what is important to them. Listening gives children status—people who are listened to are worth listening to. Unfortunately, as teachers we don't always do a good job of listening. There is so little time in the school day, and so much to cover in the curriculum. It's much easier, and more time efficient, to just tell children what they need to know. Repeatedly, research has shown that most classrooms are dominated by teacher talk, and when students do get to talk, it's in a recitation mode as they try to answer questions teachers have asked (Cazden, 1988; Dillon & Searle, 1981; Mehan, 1979). However, as literature discussion groups are incorporated in the classroom, it becomes easier to give children a chance to talk and ourselves a chance to listen.

Reflection Point

Take an audiotape recorder to class, and turn it on at a time in the day when you are having a discussion with the class or group. Position the recorder so you can capture what you and the children say, and record the duration of the conversation. Put in a new tape and record a point in the day when you are not having a discussion. Let it record the same amount of time. Later, listen to both tapes. What do you notice? Who is doing the most talking? What are the differences, if any, between discussion time and other class time? In your journal, write down what you notice.

Literature discussion groups are a perfect venue for learning to listen. You cannot conduct a successful discussion if you do not listen to what the children are saying. Notice in the following conversation how Lisa is an active and supportive listener. This was difficult at the beginning of the year because children were used to the common, school turn-taking pattern of initiation, response, and evaluation: The teacher asks a question, receives an answer, evaluates that answer, and then asks another question, repeating the cycle. In this conversation early in the school year,

Lisa is trying to get her students to talk to each other, not only to her. To do this, she has them listen carefully. Even so, the conversation is halting, often painful, and full of pauses and false starts.

It is early September and Lisa has reminded the students that they need to be ready to share. She has told them to keep their hands down—to jump into the discussion—to promote more natural conversation.

> **Lisa:** You don't have to read your response. You can just share by talking and make it your goal to say something to someone else.

Cameron begins by reading his response to Beatrice Schenk deRegnier's *May I Bring a Friend?*, telling about his favorite part. Chris raises his hand and asks a clarifying question. Lisa reminds them that they do not have to raise their hands. Cameron answers Chris and shows a picture from the book to illustrate his answer. Jasmyn is next.

Jasmyn: *Pink and Say.*

Chris: By Patricia Polacco.

Jasmyn then reads her response.

Cameron: (turning to face Jasmyn) Did you like the book?

Jasmyn: Yeah, it's interesting.

Lisa: Next response?

Cameron: Just jump in, just jump in.

Chris: (holding up his book [Anthony Browne's *Willy and Hugh*]) I think Willy is sad.

Cameron and Jasmyn raise their hands.

Cheng: Why do you think it [the book] was sad? Willy didn't think it was sad. In the book, it didn't say Willy was sad.

Lisa: Cheng, you're saying that Willy is not sad. Chris, you are saying that he is sad. How do you know?

Chris demonstrates how Willy walks sadly.

Lisa: Are you seeing he's sad in words and pictures?

Chris: Yes.

Lisa: Cheng's point is that the words do not convey the message that he is sad, just pictures. (Chris agrees.)

Lisa: That's an interesting point. So we have to consider both, don't we, in picture books? Both the pictures and the words. Good point.

| Chris: | This just reminded me of the first day of school here when I didn't have any friends. |
| Lisa: | Do others of you relate to that? |

Several hands go up, and then Pilar takes her turn.

Pilar:	*Henry and Mudge and the Careful Cousin* (by Cynthia Rylant). (She then reads her response and adds) I liked the story because the cousin got dog drool on him and he turned pink.
Chris:	Do you know why she turned pink?
Pilar:	'Cause the dog licked her.
Shida:	Why did you like that part?
Pilar:	'Cause I never saw anyone who's pink.
Jasmyn:	That girl is pink. Do you know why she turned pink?
Lisa:	Jasmyn, listen to other questions and responses so that you don't ask the same question.
Will:	I like this book.
Lisa:	Give the title of the book.
Will:	*Henry and Mudge Get the Cold Shivers* by Cynthia Rylant. I like this book because at the end Mudge was okay.
Chris:	Why did you like that part?
Will:	Because Mudge wasn't sick anymore.
Lisa:	Will, do you like happy endings? Sarah, why do you like Henry and Mudge books (a series by Cynthia Rylant)?
Will:	I don't know; because they're funny.
Lisa:	That's something to think about because a lot of you like Henry and Mudge books.
Pilar:	(asking Will) Why did you think he was okay?
Will:	Because he wasn't sick anymore.

The remainder of the discussion was similar in that students made short, comfortable responses, beginning with "I liked...," and the discussion became more a question-answer dialogue than a conversation. However, they learned to ask one another questions rather than looking to Lisa every time someone offered a response. Lisa attempted to promote conversation about Willy's feelings by getting clarification from Cheng and Chris about their responses to him, but they did not converse with each other except through her. When Chris offered a link to his own life, Lisa asked others if they related in the same way, but they responded merely by raising their hands rather than offering comments. Lisa reminded the group, with her gentle reminder to Jasmyn, to listen to what others say, and she made two other attempts to get the children to relate to what their peers were saying. With her help, they worked toward conversation. It was still early.

By listening to what her students say, Lisa lets them know that everyone should listen because what they are saying is important. Often she shows this through example, but equally often it is stated explicitly, with a positive evaluation of a student's contribution.

Cameron has his journal in hand and is ready to share Donald Crews's *Bigmama's*.

Cameron:	I liked the part in this book where they called the grandmother Bigmama.
Lisa:	They called their grandmother Bigmama? What's the name of the book? Who's the author?
Cameron:	*Bigmama's* by Donald Crews. They called her Bigmama not because she was big but because she was special. It sounds like someone loves that person.
Lisa:	You know what I liked about Cameron's response is that he's not only telling us what he liked, he's giving us a good reason. That's important.

While Lisa is praising Cameron for both his response and his reasoning, he reaches for his book, poises himself, and is ready to read a portion of the text. Lisa asks him to share.

Cameron:	This is my favorite part: "Cottondale, Cottondale..." (He reads a short segment.)
Lisa:	Why did you want to share that particular part?
Cameron:	It's funny, like a joke.

Lisa continued to praise Cameron's use of the book to clarify his enjoyment of the book and to elaborate on his response. Cameron had successfully modeled a good response and returned to the text to support his response. Lisa used this opportunity to emphasize this strategy to her students. Almost immediately, students began adopting similar strategies of returning to texts and illustrations to bridge their response and emergent reasoning. For example, Sarah and Jasmyn both read from their texts to support their points in subsequent sessions.

Lisa continues to invite her students to respond to each other, as in this conversation following a whole-group oral reading of Patricia Polacco's *Pink and Say*.

Lisa:	Just jump in, add something, ask questions.
Cameron:	I didn't like the part when Moe Moe Bay got shot. They were mean soldiers, and I think Pink and Say should have gone with the soldiers to Andersonville because then Moe Moe Bay wouldn't have died and no one would have died.
Chris:	That's a good point.
Lisa:	(to all) What do you think?
Chris:	I have a point to make. How would we know that they wouldn't have died? Pink and Say were just kids. Moe Moe Bay was old. She had lived most of her life already.
Lisa:	(turns towards Cameron) What do you think about that?
Cameron:	That's a really good point, Chris. But I don't know what to say.
Lisa:	That's okay. Sometimes, we need time to think.

From the beginning, Lisa encouraged the students to abandon the turn-taking pattern they had learned and jump right in. She created the opportunity for students' real conversations about books and their need for time to think, and for the chance to construct meaning over time.

Lisa provided supportive structures for students to learn to be active participants in discussion. In early September, she discusses a list of helpful guidelines for discussion groups, which she stapled to the students' journals for safekeeping (see Box 2-2).

Lisa:	One—Stay on topic. What does that mean?
Chris:	Stay on task. You don't just start talking about something else. Talk about the story, not what happened last night.
Lisa:	Yes, we should be talking about the story. Stay on the story. Number two—Be active in discussion. What does that mean, Will? Sarah? Shida?
Sarah:	Talking about something.
Lisa:	Yes, I want you to talk about something.

Cameron:	You can use the front page [of your journal].
Lisa:	Excellent idea, Cameron! If you don't know what to say, you can look at your sentence starters for a way to start. Number three—If you don't understand something, ask someone to explain. What can you do?
Pilar:	Ask nicely.
Lisa:	Who would like to do that for me? Pilar? Pretend I just gave a response and you don't understand.
Pilar:	Could you please discuss it again?
Lisa:	Perfect. Can you please say it again? Okay, number four—Listen carefully to what others have said. It's important that you be a good listener as well as a talker. Number five—Don't be afraid to disagree. But do it politely. Look back in the book. Number six—Give everybody a chance to share their ideas. Number seven—Be ready to support your opinions with evidence from the story. If you think something, you should be able to go back and say, "I think that because of words or pictures."

As the children got better at being members of a conversational group, Lisa began to speak less, although she continued to listen carefully. In the dialogue that follows, Lisa supports the students with real, probing questions and encourages them to create meaning collaboratively.

BOX 2-2
Student Guidelines for Discussion Groups

1. Keep the conversation going.
2. Stay on task.
3. Include all group members in the discussion.
4. Take turns.
5. Do not interrupt each other.
6. Respond to questions and ideas brought up by other members.
7. Be polite.

Created by Lisa Stanzi's students.

It is October and students have been discussing fantasy, struggling with identifying features of fantasy and distinguishing fact from fantasy. Achala has just finished *Catwings* (by Ursula Le Guin).

Achala:	*Catwings.* I know this story is not true because cats don't talk and don't have wings. I wonder how the cats got their wings.
Students:	Maybe Santa went down the chimney.
Jasmyn:	The author should have told you.
Sarah:	Yeah, at the end, like a surprise.
Chris:	This book kind of reminds me of Horton, the elephant who has the egg, because the baby was half elephant and half bird.
Lisa:	Achala, did it bother you that you didn't know how cats got their wings?
Achala:	No! I like the way cats pronounce "human beans" and what cats say when people pick them up and want to keep them.
Brett:	They have bigger wings than birds.
Lisa:	Why do they have bigger wings than birds?

Think about the turn-taking patterns in the preceding dialogue. First, Lisa's voice was absent from the first five exchanges. When she finally asked a question, several students answered, talking to each other as well as directing their answers to her. Further, her questions were real questions for which she really wanted the answers. These kinds of questions contrasted with questions to which the teacher already knew the answer or questions that were oral quizzes instead of discussion facilitators. Lisa's questions in this and other conversations encouraged students' personal connections with books, asked them to explore how the books work, and pushed them to evaluate what they were reading and made connections to what they already read. Her questions arose from the children's comments, and she listened and built on this to help expand her students' understandings.

By the end of the year, the children were carrying the discussions themselves, with Lisa as a contributing member, usually clarifying and summarizing, as in the following conversation that occurred in late April.

The group is discussing Sid Fleischman's *The Whipping Boy*, a fantasy chapter book about a spoiled but neglected young prince and the boy who serves him. The group reads the book together by reading chapters aloud in class and independently at home. They are discussing the characters of the Cutthroats, a group of scoundrels and thieves who have kidnapped the prince and his whipping boy.

Lisa: So, the author is doing a good job of characterization. Are you finding that you can predict what the Cutthroats are going to do just because you know the characters? You know that they steal. They're no good, greedy.

Cameron: Yep!

Jasmyn: They'd say, if you give me this, then I'll give you nothing.

Lisa: Sneaky, like Brett said, they'd promise you one thing and not even deliver.

Cameron: Like they can say, I'll give you this for a bunch of candy, then they give them that, then they say, "my hands are crossed."

Amarachi: I think I know why Hold Your Nose Billy smells like garlic. In Chapter 7, I noticed that Hold Your Nose Billy teases the prince again when he said, (reading from the book) "I can't write and crows can't fly."

Jasmyn: Maybe the reason they thought that was because he doesn't want to write it for him and they...

Lisa: What do you think about that teasing?

Cameron: Those Cutthroats, they're just teasy.

Pilar: They're mean.

The conversation continues as the students discuss the characteristics of a variety of unusual characters. The next day, Sarah begins the conversation:

Sarah: Why did Jemmy sign Prince Brat's name instead of his?

Jasmyn: Because Prince Horace didn't know how to write and Jemmy couldn't put his name because they didn't ask him to write the letter.

Cameron: They didn't ask who to write the letter?

Jasmyn: Jemmy

Cameron: But I think Jemmy...

Chris: Hold on. Wait a minute. In Chapter 7...

Sarah:	In Chapter 8...
Chris:	I've got to go back to Chapter 7, because I didn't read Chapter 8. (He'd been absent.) In Chapter 8, I take it, Jemmy wrote the letter, correct?
Students:	Yes.
Chris:	Well, then, I don't get your question, because it seems like it would be normal if he wrote the letter, why wouldn't he just sign it?
Sarah:	No, the prince should have written it, but he didn't know how to write or write his name, so Jemmy did it instead.
Chris:	I know, that's what I'm saying. Jemmy would have had to write it for two reasons. One, he was writing the letter, and if the Cutthroats had seen Jemmy giving it to the prince and saying, "prince, sign this," then I think they would have been a little suspicious. So it would have made just plain sense and also because the prince doesn't know how to spell, so he would have had to sign it.
Lisa:	What would they have been suspicious of?
Chris:	They would have been like, they would have, I would just think if I were Cutwater or Hold Your Nose Billy and I saw Jemmy or that they thought Jemmy was the prince and I saw the prince hand it to the Whipping Boy and say... uhh...shh...whatever he would have called him, please sign this, I think I would've gone, "Why is he getting the Whipping Boy to sign this?"
Lisa:	Did you hear that? Listen to that first part again. This is the whole part that you're missing, Sarah.

As Lisa listened to her students, she also helped them learn to listen to each other. As in the preceding discussions, she taught them to listen by

- explicitly encouraging them to respond to each other,
- summarizing what they had said,
- showing that she valued what they had to say,
- building on their comments in her responses,
- asking interesting questions that had no wrong answers,
- asking questions that furthered the children's understanding of what they were reading,

- asking questions that helped the children think about why they were responding as they did, and

- spending time talking about procedures and rules that furthered their discussions.

Reflection Point_____

Listen again to the tape of the class discussion that you made earlier. As you listen, write down the turn-taking patterns. Listen again to what you said. Were the questions asked ones to which you did not know the answer, or were they little tests in the guise of questions? Did you encourage students to talk to each other? Did your questions or comments build on the children's comments, or were they part of a pre-established routine? In your journal describe your discussion behaviors and reflect on what you could do differently. Choose one thing you'd like to change and try it the next day; write down what happened and how you felt about the experience.

Learning Tasks and Procedures

At the beginning of the year, Lisa spent time teaching children how to behave in a conversational group. Many of her turns at talk were spent directing children's behavior or scaffolding ways to discuss (Langer, 1991). She asked questions that indicated to students when they needed to discuss their responses and when they needed to be sure that they had made themselves clear to others. She also demonstrated ways they could enter into the conversation and how they could sustain discussions. She talked about body language and how looking at the speaker shows that you are paying attention and valuing what the speaker is saying. She taught them how not to interrupt and how to link what they were saying to the responses of others. She taught them the value of listening, waiting, and thinking.

As the year progressed and her students became more adept at having conversations, Lisa's turns at talk decreased and changed in focus. Rather than spending time scaffolding ways to discuss, she was spending her time on scaffolding ways to think (Langer, 1991). By the end of the year, she spent most of her time helping students learn ways to think about the books they were reading. She helped them focus, assisted them in shaping their ideas in a cohesive fashion, and showed them how to link their conversations to previous discussions, to ideas that had been presented earlier in the conversation, and to their life experiences.

In the following discussion of *The Whipping Boy*, Lisa helps her students focus on their impressions and develop their ideas about a character.

Cameron:	He's just spoiled.
Brett:	He was spoiled and afraid. He was afraid of everything.
Cameron:	Yeah, and to be alone with the Cutthroats while he...
Lisa:	So, him being spoiled means what, Cameron?
Chris:	I think he's just afraid. I'd be afraid, too. I wouldn't want to be left alone with two ugly, one fat, and one skinny Cutthroat.
Lisa:	So it's his fear, you're saying?
Chris:	Yeah.
Lisa:	So it's his fear that drove him to give Jemmy away?

Listening closely and helping children clarify their thinking with questions enabled Lisa to help these second-grade readers move beyond a simple statement about character traits to a thoughtful consideration of a character's feelings and motives. Listening well and knowing our students also allows us to help them shape their initial ideas, often fragmentary, into cohesive thoughts that can be shared with and understood by others.

Pilar:	It's going very, very slow like and then the airplane gets fast. It's very, very slow.
Lisa:	So there has to be that building of trust?
Pilar:	Jemmy's trying to believe that he can trust Prince Brat because Prince Brat is trying to be like him, and he's trying to trust him, that Prince Brat can be just like him.

This brief exchange illustrates what keen listeners teachers must be. Lisa knew Pilar well and could support her initial comment, which at first glance seems rather bizarre, by considering the significance of Jemmy's feelings. Attentive listening and a good memory also helped Lisa link students' comments to previous discussions, ideas, and experiences.

> **Lisa:** So don't forget how we need to think about those things that are going on in the story, and why he would feel that way, and what you think will happen because of this.

Later in the same discussion, she helps students link their knowledge to the structure of the text:

> **Lisa:** I just glanced down at Chapter 7 and thought, wait a minute. I don't see that [event] happening. It doesn't seem right. So remember, if you're going to make a statement, make sure you base it on what actually happened in the story, not what you think happened or would like to happen.

Lisa also reminds students of previous discussions.

> **Lisa:** This idea sounds familiar. Yes. We've talked about this before.

Her explicit linking with past discussions, knowledge of text structure, and previous experiences with literature helped her students think about reading and discussing books as a connected, rather than isolated, activity. Students adopted these ways of connecting and soon used them to explore texts without any prompting from Lisa.

Lisa's constant listening, rephrasing, summarizing, and nudging often resulted in her students gaining new and deeper understandings about characters, about literature, and about life. Her support allowed children to step out of the story world and think about what they knew to be true in the world they experienced (Langer, 1995).

In the following conversation, the students talk about Prince Brat, still contemplating why he acts the way he does:

> **Lisa:** What did we learn, though, in Chapter 14 about the relationship between Prince Brat and his father?
>
> **Cameron:** That his father never really noticed Prince Brat before.
>
> **Lisa:** There was a line that Prince Brat said while having a discussion with Jemmy, and it was like.... Oh, and it was like

a window into the relationship between Prince Brat and his father. And when I was reading that I thought, hmm-mm, maybe that's why he doesn't want to go back.

Chris: Because his father never does anything. His father never notices him. He's like, he's a shadow.

Lisa: What does that mean, notice?

Sarah: He didn't, like, really play with him or anything like our dads do.

Jasmyn: Like when he wanted to play something his father tells him he's busy or not right now or something.

Chris: Prince Brat knows how to play stuff, like pulling off people's wigs.

Lisa: So then what is he missing?

Chris: His father.

Sarah: He doesn't quite have a real father.

Brett: His father is king and he has too much to do, and he can't do much with the prince.

Chris: He is a real father, but...

Sarah: He doesn't seem like what a father would be.

Lisa: Okay, so are you saying that Prince Brat is just spoiled and he's expecting too much out of his dad?

Cameron: Yes.

Brett: He's too busy to pay attention.

Chris: I guess the reason that he's always being a brat is because he...

Sarah: He wants attention.

Cameron: He wants to get attention.

Brett: He never gets any love from his father.

Lisa: What did you say, Brett?

Brett: He never gets any love from his father.

Lisa: So, it's not that he's a spoiled brat?

Sarah: No.

Lisa: He's missing something?

Sarah: He never gets cuddles like we do from our dads and moms.

Lisa: That's affection, isn't it? So are you thinking that Prince Brat thinks that no one cares about him?

Sarah:	He doesn't care about anybody else because nobody else cares about him.
Lisa:	I see. So you're saying that if we didn't get love and affection then it would be hard for us to care about other people.
Chris:	And I think the reason that Jemmy is opposite of Prince Brat is he had a father. His father was never like, "I'm way too busy to do anything with you."
Sarah:	Yeah, they catch rats together.
Jasmyn:	But the prince, his father didn't really do that much.
Lisa:	What do you mean? He had everything he wanted!
Sarah:	Except for love.
Jasmyn:	He had everything he wanted, but everything he wanted wasn't enough to satisfy him.
Cameron:	He just wanted his dad.
Lisa:	You mean all the clothes, all the toys, having a whipping boy, all that stuff?
Cameron:	He wanted love from his dad.
Jasmyn:	That stuff is nice, but he needs his father more than he needs all that.
Lisa:	So, you're saying that Jemmy had more than the prince did?
Sarah:	Uh huh. He had more love.
Lisa:	He was poor. He didn't even get anything to eat.
Sarah:	Love, attention.
Cameron:	He gets more attention from his dad, the rat catcher.
Lisa:	So wait a minute. Are you saying that the love overruled even the hunger and the food? He didn't have toys and he didn't have a mom and all that stuff?
Jasmyn:	You need your dad more than you need all that junk.
Brett:	You need your parents.
Sarah:	And mom.
Jasmyn:	You need mom and dad.
Sarah:	You need love, cuddling, attention.
Lisa:	You could just have one. It could be one or the other.

Jasmyn:	Like I could just have my mother. (Jasmyn's mother is a single parent.)
Cameron:	My mom's a single mom.
Lisa:	Exactly. And you're very empathetic to other people. That means you've gotten lots of love and you love other people.
Jasmyn:	Like, you love your whole family.
Lisa:	Interesting. Amarachi, what do you think about all this?
Sarah:	I say I think it's cool.
Lisa:	What's cool?
Sarah:	The way we just explained about...
Brett:	You [Lisa] were trying to convince us that all the toys were enough but we changed. That was better.
Jasmyn:	It is better.
Sarah:	We're some kids.
Amarachi:	I agree, because my mom keeps on saying that love is the greatest thing that you could ever get.

They are, indeed, "some kids," and they go on to discuss why they think that Prince Brat is changing, and return to the text to prove their points.

It is important to understand, however, that there was not some magical line that Lisa and her students crossed that told her to focus on how to think about what they were reading. Instruction in how to discuss and how to think were present from the beginning of the year. By listening to and learning from her students as they talked about the books they read, Lisa made decisions about what they needed help with at various moments, knowing that there were other conversations that would allow her to teach them the many other things they needed to know.

Recall the journal entry that Lisa wrote following the drizzly November conversation (see page 2). Here's what she wrote in April:

> What a great discussion! Amarachi shared with the class about why to look through the faraway end, which was extraordinary in itself, and that led to a discussion of Patricia MacLachlan's *Arthur, for the Very First Time* and how some books stick with you. (They had last read this book in January.) Chris commented something to the effect that "some books are better than others and some books you read more deeply. Like we read, we read more deeply than most people. We think about what hap-

pened, but also why it happened." I tried to act calm and cool on the outside, but I was bursting with joy on the inside. I could barely look at Lee; we both knew what an incredible conversation this was. It was so hard to focus on the conversation, because I wanted to shout, this is fabulous stuff! Shida read his first Asian tale last night. Sarah had read it the previous night and she gave it rave reviews. I've been wondering why he hadn't read any of the Asian tales I put in the basket. Amarachi responded to Pilar! Yes! These kids constantly amaze me.

*Reflection Point*_____

Audiotape another conversation about books and listen to it, tallying each instance in which you are teaching your students how to discuss, and in which you are teaching your students how to think about what they are reading. What things are you showing them how to do? What else might you have been able to teach them during that particular conversation? What else do you need to keep in mind as you continue to discuss books with them? What else do they need to learn? What are they doing that amazes you?

_____

Learning to Self-Monitor

One of the things this group needed to learn was how to monitor themselves as members of a group. Lisa did this by asking them to think about how they were discussing books, and by asking them to listen and to view themselves on audiotape and on videotape. After school resumed following the winter break, conversational skills were almost as shaky as they had been at the beginning of the year. Troubled by what she saw, Lisa decided to let her students hear and see themselves just as she had done. In early January Lisa felt that they needed to spend structured time learning how to reflect on and monitor their behavior. Although she did this kind of instruction in the beginning of the year through her own demonstrations, here she explicitly asks students to reflect in systematic ways:

Lisa: Today, we will begin by stepping back and reflecting. Yesterday, I said it would be a good idea if we listened to our conversations. When I went back and listened to our discussion, it was hard to hear all the conversation. We really need to project our voices. That's what we need to think about. We are not listening to this to pick on anyone. We should respect each other. The purpose of doing this is to reflect on ourselves and the tone of our voices. We should also think about "What did I add to the discussion?" or "Am I really saying something interesting?" Also, focus on the positive. What do we do well? What and how can we improve?

The students engage in discussion, which Lisa records. After the discussion is completed, Lisa puts the video into the VCR for the students to view their participation. Lisa passes out paper.

Lisa: When you think of things we did well or things we need to improve, write it down.

Lisa begins playing the tape. Students are generally attentive and make notes on their papers. Some giggle at seeing themselves, but overall, the tone of the group is serious. When the tape is finished, Lisa turns to the group:

Lisa: What did you notice?

Brett: We need to know what we want to say before we say it. Sarah started saying, "ummmm." We need to know.

Chris: (to Sarah) We are not saying you are doing a bad job.

Lisa: That's a good point. We need to be rehearsed. Not only are you doing your response, but what relevant things can you bring to the group—the most interesting things? What's going to provide and promote discussion?

All the students talk at once.

Maria: I don't think we should talk at the same time.

Jasmyn: We can improve on controlling our talking.

Lisa: Not only can we improve on talking, but also on listening. Let's focus on what we are saying.

Sarah: Will didn't understand it.

Brett: He's not understanding.

Maria: And lots of people were correcting Sarah.

Brett: Think about what you say before you say it.

Lisa:	What else?
Pilar:	Everybody was talking at once.
Lisa:	What did we do well?
Brett:	We were speaking up.
Lisa:	Yes.
Brett:	The person who we are talking to, we need to look at that person.
Cameron:	You can be shy, but you have to speak up.

Lisa plays more of the tape and then stops again for discussion.

Lisa:	Who is doing the majority of the talking?
Students:	Sarah.
Lisa:	Why do you think?
Pilar:	Everybody did the same amount.
Lisa:	Everybody? You may want to think about that some more. Who is an active listener? Are you really participating in the discussion? Why am I not saying anything? Why do people choose not to say anything?
Cheng:	We still have to wait for someone to stop talking or it wouldn't be clear.
Brett:	We should try not to correct people.

Chris agrees with Brett, and Maria says that's what she has written down, too. Jasmyn recalls being corrected and several students agree with nods.

Lisa:	Maybe we need to be more sensitive to one another. Keep thinking about how you can improve. How are we going to improve?

The next morning, Lisa begins the discussion by reminding students of the group evaluation from the previous day.

Lisa:	We are going to be working on...
Maria:	Don't speak when someone else is speaking.
Lisa:	Yes, watch the overlaps.
Cheng:	Speaking up.
Pilar:	Listening.
Brett:	Have [eye] contact.

Lisa continues the practice of reviewing the group's processes and discussing what was working and what was not. In February, Lisa shows another clip of video for students to evaluate.

Lisa:	Let's talk about ourselves.
Will:	I am fumbling around.
Lisa:	Do you notice that certain people are talking more than others? Are you aware of it?
Jasmyn:	We're responding a lot.
Lisa:	Did anyone else notice anything? Some of you really are not aware. Seeing the video helps. You can bring it to a conscious level.
Jasmyn:	Do not interrupt each other.
Lisa:	What else?
Chris:	People kept interrupting each other.
Jasmyn:	We kept three conversations going.
Sarah:	Amarachi didn't talk.
Lisa:	Maria asked Amarachi a question, "Did she read that book yesterday?" In order to know when to jump in, you have to be in it.
Jasmyn:	Everybody might just sit there.
Lisa:	Anything else? What were we doing right?
Chris:	We were being polite.
Jasmyn:	We were staying on task. We responded to questions.
Lisa:	Give me an example.
Jasmyn:	When Brett said she liked Howie.
Chris:	I disagree with that because you [Lisa] had to come out and ask.
Lisa:	Based on what we have seen, what do we need to work on?
Brett:	We need to speak up.
Pilar:	Keep the conversation going.
Lisa:	I think we need you [Pilar] in it. You weren't with us. Did you notice that?

Such sessions seemed to be a turning point in the class as their discussion skills re-emerged and they tried to monitor their behaviors on the spot. After these discussions, Lisa created and displayed a chart to re-mind students how to discuss. Almost daily, Lisa encouraged and re-minded students to self-monitor and reflect on their thinking and behavior, which is critical for successful participation in literature discus-sions. Perhaps it would have been easier for Lisa to tell students what to do. Instead, she invited them to reflect on themselves and to take respon-sibility for the success of each day's discussion. She shuttled back and forth between the roles of teacher and discussion participant as needed. Lisa's responsiveness to students' inquiry through literature made this kind of self-assessment possible.

By turning the responsibility for the group's behavior over to the group through teaching them to self-monitor and reflect, Lisa helped her students grow as members of that particular community. Their re-sponsibility was to themselves and to the other members of the group, and they worked to live up to that responsibility. Group pressure helped everyone behave as good conversational partners would. Lisa, gradually freed of the responsibility of managing the group's behavior, was then free to focus on what the children were revealing about themselves as read-ers and as people as they participated in the group discussions.

Learning to Use Journals as Preparation for Discussion

From the beginning of the year, the literature group wrote in journals (small, blue exam books), which were replaced as soon as they were filled. These journals served many functions, one of which was to prepare the children to talk about books with each other, linking reading, writing, and discussion. Lisa provided ideas for writing or prompts (see Box 2-3 on page 34) on the inside cover of each journal, and initially the children all relied on those prompts as they sought to become comfortable writing about what they were reading.

The early journal entries reflected both the students' reliance on the prompts and their lack of fluency in this new task (entries are reprinted as written):

BOX 2-3
Journal Prompts

I thought of…

I noticed…

If I were…

I can't believe…

My favorite character is…

I felt ___ when…

This made me think of…

The problem here is…

I disliked…

Sometimes I'm not sure about…

It seemed like real life when…

Now I understand…

I'm confused about…

I wonder what will happen if…

I think the author's reason for writing this book was…

I love the way…

I wonder why…

I think…

I'm not sure…

I like the way the author…

I wish that…

Something I learned was…

If I were in this story…

The setting of the story…

The way I think a certain character looks is…

If I were writing this story I…

The funniest part is…

I hope that…

This reminds me of something in my own life…

The character most like me is…

From Hirsch, K. (1997). I can't be like Pippi 'cause I'm afraid to live alone: Third graders' response to novels. In N.J. Karolides (Ed.), *Reader response in elementary classrooms*. Mahwah, NJ: Erlbaum.

9-2-97 Matthew and tilly

dy Rebecca Jones

It raminds me of my life Because sometimes I git in fights with my fieinds. (Chris)

9-3-97 henry and Mudge get the cold shivers

I thot the story was funny becuase when Mudge woke up and wasn't sick

he sloBers all over henry. (Chris)

Big Mamas by Donald Crews 9-4-97

I like the part When they acall ther gradMother Big Mama it sound like someones in love. (Cameron)

9-8-97 The letter by Arnold Lobel

I liked the story because It show friedship. I know it because frog wirtes toad a letter. Toad was very happy. It is a very happy story. It is funny to. (Maria)

9-2-97 Matthew and tilly

by Rebecca C. Jones

My favorite character is tilly because shared a lot of things with matthew. (Amarachi)

9-4-97 Pink and say

patricia Polocco

I didn't really understand it but it made me think of something. I made me think about friendship because Pink and Say were friends. Just like me and xxx are friends. (Achala)

9-4-97 pink and say

By patrieia Polacco

I think that story was grate infaakt this is one of the Best Books iyv ever red the end. (Sarah)

9-8-97 Pink and say

by patricia polacco

I didn't like the part were they killed moe moe Bay Cause she had worked very very hard for pink and say and she did'nt deserve to die. Because she was very old and she was a nice lady. thats all (Jasmyn)

9-11-97 All I see By Cyntha ryant

This reminds me of when I got a Brush and another Brush and I staed paning. It was so fun. I got to wabe my pateBrush all I wat to. (Pilar)

9-16-97 Mr. Putter and Tabby Pour the tea [a book by Cynthia Rylant]

1. Mr. Putter I wonder why Mr. Putter was all alone. Mr. Putter is nice because he look nice. 2. Tabby. Tabby looks poor. Why does Tabby take bath in the garden? 3. Mr. Putter and Tabby. I think the storys was great because they Live together. They shared wonderful things.   (Shida)

Initially, the prompts and resulting responses found their way into the conversation, just as Lisa's oral remarks found their way into the children's repertoire. In the early discussions presented throughout this chapter, you can hear the students begin their contributions with the ideas for written prompts that Lisa had provided. They knew she valued these ideas because she had given them the prompts, and they wanted to please her. Unfortunately, ideas did not translate well from writing to talking as each child read his or her journal entry in a round-robin fashion, without any connection to a previous contribution.

By asking children to do other things, Lisa provided alternatives to the cycle of reading individually, writing in the journal, and sharing. They were invited to read a story with a partner, discuss the story, and write a response, then exchange responses with the partner, read the partner's response, and write a response to the partner. The results looked much like the following entry, taken from Sarah's journal in October 1997, which was written after reading Simon James's *Dear Mr. Blueberry* with Amarachi.

Dear Mr. Blueberry

A real whale could not live in a little pond. It would be inpossilble for a whale.

Would it be inpossilble for a elephant or a kangaroo?   (Amarachi)

A kangaroo could. But not an elephant!   (Sarah)

As time went on, the children began to learn that journal writing was a time to rehearse what they might want to discuss later, and to write down "wonderings" and questions that occurred to them as they read. These questions and wonderings began to initiate extended conversation. Initially, Lisa worried that wonderings were a waste of time, leading nowhere. As she listened and reflected, however, she came to see that they were, indeed, valuable attempts by her students to understand what they were reading in terms of their own lives and experiences, and to make sense of what was happening in both life and texts.

Sometimes the discussions prompted the children to write about particular things in their journals. One day, during a discussion of Patricia MacLachlan's *Sarah, Plain and Tall*, a brief novel about a young woman who travels west to become the wife and mother in a prairie family, the children noticed that the author had not used chapter titles as she had in *Arthur, for the Very First Time*, which they had previously read and discussed. This discussion prompted a spate of journal entries that included naming the chapters as they read them, and supporting their decision about appropriate titles. These journal entries, in turn, became catalysts for discussion. Below is a dialogue from one such discussion.

Will offers "Old Singing Days" as a possible title for the first chapter, which is followed by suggestions for other possibilities.

> **Pilar:** Seasons.
>
> **Lisa:** Remember it. What do you think based on words, the feelings?
>
> **Jasmyn:** The one I have for Chapter 2 is "The Writer."
>
> **Lisa:** Let's talk about Chapter 2.

Students continue to offer possibilities for other chapters in subsequent discussions. Title possibilities for Chapter 3 focus on the sea. For Chapter 4, many students say "summer" and "singing."

> **Lisa:** Oh, I can tell you are all thinking as you're reading. When do you think of the title?

Some students say "after reading" and others say "during" their reading of the chapter.

> **Chris:** I usually get it from the beginning or the end.
>
> **Sarah:** I have to read and then decide.
>
> **Cameron:** Yes, and sometimes it's hard to choose.

In naming the chapters, more often than not students have different suggestions for titles, which momentarily worries some of them, so they discuss it.

> **Will:** I don't think my chapter names are good because they are different than everybody else's.

Jasmyn:	That's what makes it fun.
Cameron:	It doesn't really matter.
Lisa:	Wouldn't it be boring if everyone came up with the same title? So, what did you name it?
Will:	Summer Singing.

They have a brief discussion about Will's title, and Lisa tells him to go with what he feels about chapter titles. She praises everyone for supporting him.

As you can see, thinking about titles for individual chapters became a wonderful vehicle for summarizing, discussing theme, and talking about main ideas.

Although writing in journals and talking in the group were always linked, Lisa attempted to move the children from a total reliance on their journals as conversational starters to using them as reminders of some of the things they were thinking as they were reading. Asking them to look quickly at their journals and then put them under their chairs helped free the children from relying entirely on what they had written. However some managed for quite a while to hold a book, look at the other members of the group, and read from their journal on the floor all at the same time!

Sometimes journals were used to record thoughts and feelings after discussions, especially when the children worked together in pairs or groups before coming together for a literature-group discussion. In these instances, the journals served as a record of what the smaller group had talked about or how ideas had changed.

Maria, Brett, and Chris are in a small group discussing Steven Kellogg's *The Mysterious Tadpole*.

Chris:	I see a problem here, page 334 [*Literature Works*, second-grade level]. Alphonse is in the bathroom and it looks like he's breaking everything. I wonder where they got the money to fix that.
Brett:	I think they used (inaudible) to fix it.
Chris:	(deduces that they would not have enough money) I think it's weird that Louis has that dream and the sign says "Danger, Beware" and Alphonse is laying down crying. You're supposed to be scared of that.
Maria:	(Inaudible.)

Brett:	I wonder how Alphonse could smell the awful smell. I wonder how he could see under the water.
Lisa:	I hear you saying there was lots of humor in this story.
Brett:	Louis's parents didn't want him to go and wanted the bird.
Chris:	Maybe they didn't. How do you know? It doesn't say they kept the bird. It just says they had the bird at their house.
Lisa:	What are you going to write about in your journals?
Brett:	The humor in the story.
Maria:	The same as Brett.
Lisa:	How does the humor make the story? Is it important to the story?
Chris:	In all of my stories I put humor in my stories.
Lisa:	Steven Kellogg is the author and illustrator. How does he do it, through the words or the illustrations?
Brett:	Mostly the illustrations.

The students all come together again and tell each other what they have talked about. They then go off to write in their individual journals. The entries (reprinted as written) for Brett, Maria, and Chris read as follows:

12-18-97

I wish that I had a pet like Alphonse because he got a whole tresure chest. I wonder how Alphonse grew bigger instead on turning into a frog.
(Brett)

1-5-98

I think that there was more humor in the pitchures than words. I think Uncle McAllister and Louis had a lot in comin. I think that it's funny on page 335 when it shows Alphonse dreaming that he's eating a chesebuger twice the size of him.
(Brett)

1-4-98

On page 350 I think it's funny that a girl has white hair. This story fit's our them because it has humor and imagenary events. On page 341 why doen't the coach git the tadpole out of the 1pool then? On page 347 I think that the whater looks too shalo to be thea ocean maybe a lake but not an ocean.
(Chris)

1-5-98

I think the humor in this is in the pitucres some is in the words. But more is in the pitucres. If I had a tadpole like Alphonse I would keep him in my back yard. Becase my back yard is enormous. But Alphonse could never fit in my tub.

(Maria)

Reflection Point

Collect and read the student journals to see the ways in which students are responding. Are they using the same formula for response each time? Have you provided them with examples of alternative formats? Do you need to nudge them to try varied ways of responding? Think about the functions that journals serve in your classroom. Are they a means for you to keep track of who is reading what? Are they written preparation for oral discussion, longer written pieces, or other projects? Are they a way of linking home and school? Think about other functions you might want journals to serve. Write about this and how you might go about changing the role of journals in your classroom.

Throughout the year, the journal entries got longer and more complex. As the children learned strategies for thinking and talking about books, they increased their range of approaches to books through writing, as well as through discussion. The prompts didn't change. Rather, the children incorporated into their journals what they discussed. Consider, for example, the growth in Sarah's responses between early September and mid-March:

9-8-97

"The Letter" by Arnold Lobel (*Frog and Toad*). I like the story bekaose they are very very very funny. The end.

I go with My Family to grandmas By riki Levinson Diane goode. I like it Because at ferst thaer were three the end.

> 3-16-98
>
> Chapter 12 (of Patricia MacLachlan's *Skylark*)
>
> The Realef for Calub, Sarah and Anna
>
> I love this parte, when she gose skiny diping. I hope the drought was over. I rely rely rely hope the drought is over. It is like there is a happy momont then a very sad momont. I even forgot that Anna and Calub were not at home.

> 3-16-98
>
> chapter 13
>
> The Tears
>
> I would hate to be Calub, because he was cring like crazy. I do not like cring. Do you?

Sarah's journal entries in March read as though she were having a conversation with another reader. They show passion, engagement, and an emotional connection to the characters and their situation. These thoughts are shaped by months of reading and talking together and of trying ways of responding in the company of others.

When Chris remarked, "Here we read differently. We think about what we read," he put it well, indeed. In Lisa's classroom, the children did think about what they read, which wasn't necessarily the case at the beginning of the year, as you have seen. As they read and discussed books in the literature group, they learned how to think, write, and talk about books through the many opportunities that Lisa offered them. Some of these opportunities, such as the journal prompts, were planned as general strategies that the children could access at any time across the school year. Others, such as naming chapters, were opportunities that arose as a result of a particular book and a specific conversation. Both kinds of opportunities were important to the children in a variety of ways.

Encouraging Comparison

Lisa also employed several common strategies to encourage her students to compare the books they read. Building connections across books was something that Lisa felt was important for her students as readers and thinkers. The dialogue in this chapter demonstrates that they were, in fact, making these intertextual connections. Lisa encouraged this through specific strategies, such as using Venn diagrams to compare and contrast books (see Chapter 3), and through her demonstrations of connections that she made, her support of connections the students made, and her questions that pushed them to make connections.

Cameron was one of the first students to make intertextual connections and, once he realized that it was a valued and valuable thing to do, he made them frequently. In mid-November, as the group discussed *Arthur, for the Very First Time*, they talked about how the two characters, Arthur and Moira, were sick to their stomachs because they had consumed a bottle of what grown-ups called "tonic" and gotten drunk. Sarah mentioned the cookies that Moira made and laughed about how hard they were, when Cameron chimed in, "This reminds me of *The Adventures of Sugar and Junior* (a story by Angela Medearis they had read earlier) when the cookies were hard and they used them for rocks!"

Cameron was also one of the first to make connections to other conversations, as when he remarked to Sarah later in this same discussion, "Sarah, when you were saying you wouldn't want to lose Pauline (which she had done in a discussion earlier in the week), I wouldn't want to lose Bernadette."

Lisa rewarded him for his connections with appreciative comments ("Good for you, Cameron!"), and drew attention to what he had done by asking the rest of the class, "Did you hear what Cameron just said? He said that this reminded him of *Sugar and Junior*. Did anyone else think that? Did it remind you of anything else?"

Lisa also made connections of her own to demonstrate to the group that, as a reader herself, she found this a valuable practice. Often, she would invite the children to make the same connection as she does in a December discussion of Arthur Dorros's *Abuela*, in which a grandmother and granddaughter fly over the city on a magical journey.

> **Cameron:** The grandmother's dress was like a sail and she could race with sailboats.
>
> **Lisa:** This reminds me of another book. What might it be?
>
> **Cameron:** *The Wreck of the Zephyr*!

The children continue to discuss the illustrations of the grandmother flying in *Abuela*, comparing it to Chris Van Allsburg's *The Wreck of the Zephyr*, which they had read and discussed earlier.

As the year progressed and the children were able to compare books more easily, their conversations indicated that often one book reminded them of others they had read. These connections among books were signs of the children's development of a concept of literature as an interconnected web of stories, poems, and expository texts, not just a string of individual books. These kinds of connections began early in the year and became very common, thanks, in part, to Cameron and his wonderful ability to find links across many books. After late fall, it was a rare discussion that did not contain at least one connection between the focal text and something else they had read. These connections were to be a rich part of their responses to *The Whipping Boy* in April. The students also made connections between the books they were reading and their real-life experiences and knowledge.

While discussing *The Whipping Boy*, Brett mentions dumpsters, and Lisa asks for elaboration:

Lisa: Brett, you were saying something about dumpsters?

Brett: I was thinking about now-a-days.

Lisa: Yeah, but what about now, relate it to now.

Brett: Because some people don't have enough money to go buy food so they have to take food from the dumpsters.

Lisa: Right. When you're hungry and you have no money, and people need food in order to live, you will do whatever you can do to get food, and certainly we waste a lot of food. And going into a dumpster is one way to eat. You're right, Brett.

Brett: Like the homeless.

In a previous discussion of the novel (see page 21), the children drew on their experiences with their parents to discuss the importance of love. Both Jasmyn and Cameron, children of single mothers, remarked how a mother's love is just as important as a father's. They also made connections to other books in order to compare genres. Just a few days later, students considered how *The Whipping Boy* fit into the Stories-Around-the-World theme they were studying, comparing the novel to folktales they had been reading. The next day, Sarah linked a chapter-opening drawing to the illustrations in one of the folktales. It seemed that once the idea of connections was introduced, the students relied on this strategy regularly.

Building on Comments and Speculations

Early in the year Lisa noticed that her students had many comments and questions about the texts they were reading. Some of these questions related to understanding the content and were immediately addressed by Lisa and other students who could help clarify any lapses in comprehension. (This is discussed further in Chapter 3.) Other questions and comments at first seemed disjointed, leading to individually shared commentary but no real discussion or connections. However, when she listened intently, Lisa realized that these statements related to students' attempts to connect their own life knowledge with what was occurring in the book, most often with what the characters were doing and saying. Further, they often led to students making connections among texts, connections to the more abstract literary knowledge that they were developing, and connections between the books they were reading and their own lives. In the following discussion, Cheng adopts a letter format in an attempt to make a connection to the text.

Cheng:	Dear Arthur, why is it so hard to pick a room when the book said that? Why is everything your business? [The text] said that everything is his business. Uncle Wrisby said that it's not your business. I think it's weird.
Jasmyn:	He may want to know more.

At this point, the children move to a discussion of writing in journals. Jasmyn bridges the preceeding discussion with writing in journals, making a powerful life-to-text connection:

Jasmyn:	You are both wanting to know more. Arthur wants to know more about moles, and you want to know more about Arthur.

Jasmyn's connection between the group's experience of writing in journals to discover what they know and Arthur's journal writing is crucial to the children's understanding of Arthur's habit of writing in his journal.

Later in a discussion of the same book, the group discusses how the story is realistic. Lisa shows them one way to comment on the realism:

Lisa:	Boys can be 10 years old.
Will:	A chicken can peck at their feet.

| Pilar: | And some animals can understand, a cat or chicken, can understand French or something if they are trained. |
| Lisa: | I would talk to my dog. She wouldn't talk back to me. |

These comments show how the group would take their knowledge of the world and apply it to their understandings of the text in order to determine the reality of that text. At other times, comments might lead to a life generalization:

Lisa:	What is he doing for Bernadette?
Chris:	Making a pen.
Lisa:	What else is he doing?
Cameron:	Reading a book.
Lisa:	He's reading about her.
Pilar:	If you want to learn about something, you need to get information.

In this brief exchange, Lisa ensures that her students have understood the import of Arthur's actions, and Pilar has taken these understandings to a new height. The discussion proceeds:

Lisa:	He's getting a different perspective.
Chris:	Now he's learning that all the stuff on the outside doesn't matter. He's learning that she may look ugly but that doesn't mean she is really ugly on the inside. She is really nice on the inside.
Cheng:	Yeah, but why would a pig be like that?
Lisa:	Different on the inside than the outside? Would you like to just be judged by what we see on the outside?
Cheng:	But why would Bernadette be like that?
Lisa:	Be like what?
Cheng:	Be ugly on the outside and not ugly on the inside. I don't know what not ugly on the inside means.
Lisa:	What does that mean?
Chris:	She's nice on the inside. If you peeled off her skin, yeah, she'd still be ugly, but on the inside she's loving and caring—that kind of inside.

Cheng's wonderings elicited an explanation from Chris that spoke to the heart of both the story and life. Lisa's willingness to build on the comments and questions of her students allowed many of them to make powerful connections and build important insights. It also acknowledged that the students' own, personal responses, no matter how vague and muddled, were the foundation of the group discussions. This is certainly true of one discussion of *The Whipping Boy* in late April.

Brett:	I wonder if the Prince will ever go back to the castle.
Chris:	Probably so. I think they'll both go back.
Maria:	I don't think so.
Sarah:	I wouldn't go back. I thought Jemmy was going back to the streets. I thought he was.
Chris:	It never said he would.
Sarah:	I thought he was.
Lisa:	What do you mean, you thought he was?
Sarah:	I thought he was because...
Lisa:	Why did you think he was, Sarah? Go ahead and explain that a little bit.
Sarah:	I think he said later in the book that I will probably be going to the streets.
Lisa:	Okay, so who are you responding to, somebody saying Jemmy was going to the castle?
Sarah:	Actually, I heard...you know, when they were on the horse and the Cutthroats grabbed him, you know, "Here's my chance to go to the...to leave and go to the streets."
Lisa:	Okay, so you're talking about Chapter 15.
Sarah:	Yeah, and later on, too.
Lisa:	Okay. Brett, you asked what? You asked a good question.
Brett:	Will Prince Brat ever go back to the castle? It's like he's speaking to Jemmy.
Lisa:	Why did you ask that?
Brett:	It's like he's annoying Jemmy and he can't leave Jemmy.
Chris:	I would say definitely yes.
Lisa:	You think he's going to go back to the castle?
Brett:	I hope.
Sarah:	And I hope he's the one that gets whipped.
Chris:	I'm sorry, but I have a whole lot of doubt about that!

Jasmyn:	We all want it to happen, but it's probably not going to happen.
Brett:	The chances are slim to none.
Sarah:	Very slim.

This beginning led to the exploration of the lack of love in Prince Brat's life that was presented earlier. From small questions, great discussions grew.

Students learned that one powerful way to respond to what they read was to make a connection with their own lives, with other texts they had read, and with their growing understandings of literature. Crucial to their ability to make these connections were the initial comments, questions, speculations, and wonderings they posed. Comments made by students and Lisa helped bridge an initial response, which very often developed and elicited more sophisticated responses. Lisa's role was critical in the ways she modeled, nudged, supported, and allowed students multiple opportunities to engage in talk about texts. Her students benefited from the guidance of a more knowledgeable reader and from one another as they made their way through text toward connections.

Lisa promoted connections in other ways also, by selecting books that made connections both within and across themes.

Selecting Books

The children and Lisa were obligated to use the basal program that the school system had selected, a multicultural, literature-based reading-language arts program. Interestingly, although the materials were packaged much like the materials the students had used in first grade, they never once referred to them as "the basal" or their "reading books." Instead, they were the "literature books," and were treated as such. In Lisa's room the basal materials became another resource for reading material, equivalent to the many books in plastic bins that the children choose among for take-home reading and, later, the novels that they read together.

Reflection Point

Look at the material that you are required to use by your school district. As you look through the student material (not the teacher's guide), think about books that you might add to the basal reading material. Then look in the teacher's guide for lists of additional, related titles. Visit the school library and your local public library and ask the librarians for help locating titles to add. Visit http://www.amazon.com and browse their lists. Record new titles and authors in your journal, organizing them in a way that best suits your reading program, then jot notes about how you might use these books. It's okay to start small; adding only a few books as read-alouds may be the beginning of a wonderful change.

The basal materials were organized into six themes, and the second-grade teachers had agreed to spend approximately 6 weeks per theme, going in order throughout the year. What they did within each theme, however, varied among teachers. Lisa used the theme as an organizing principle: Add a large number of trade books to the basal, and provide time for work on a culminating project, ranging from art projects to plays to videotapes, for each theme. The trade books were take-home reading, read alouds, and small-group reading, as were the basals. They varied across genres and reading levels, and across picture-book and novel formats.

For example, in the theme on friends and family, Lisa added 50 books for the students to take home. She read aloud seven additional picture books and two poems. (The books for each theme are listed in Appendix A.) She found these books by thinking about the books she knew and owned, going to school and public libraries and talking with the librarians, and consulting resources in children's literature, some of which are listed in Box 2-4.

By adding trade books to the basal literature, Lisa was able to provide materials that enhanced the study of the theme and met the varied reading abilities of her students. Trade books provided a broader, more intensive coverage of ideas presented in the theme. Children were able to read what interested them, compare and contrast readings, and learn from each other.

The general routine was balanced among activities: Lisa reading aloud a picture book or novel, the children writing in response, then discussing it either that day or the next; the group reading a piece in a literature book or a chapter in a novel together, either aloud or silently or in pairs or small groups, writing, then discussing; and the children taking a book home, reading alone or with a family member, then telling the others about it during literature group.

Individual and Shared Knowledge

These varied reading experiences forced the children to consider what was common knowledge, held by the group as a whole, and what was individual knowledge, which should be shared with the group. This also encouraged individuals to bring their knowledge to the group to make sense of texts, as seen in the following December discussion in which Cameron shares his take-home book, Anthony Browne's *Gorilla* (1985):

Cameron: I thought the gorilla was gonna rule the world cause this one up on the roof was playing with airplanes. And I thought that Hannah got a new one for her birthday, because of this gorilla right here.

Lisa shows the group the illustrations and points out that the gorilla is in the audience.

Lisa: Did anyone notice that before?

Cameron: And I thought that he was the gorilla.

Lisa:	What do you mean by he? You've got to explain fully because you've read the story and others might not have.
Cameron:	I thought that Hannah's dad was the gorilla, but she got a new gorilla for her birthday, and if you squeeze it, it will talk a little.
Lisa:	Who else has read this story and would like to add?

Shida volunteers that he hadn't noticed the gorilla in the audience. Lisa notes that when Maria shared this book, Pilar noticed something.

Lisa:	It seems like we're seeing multiple layers here. Is there a fantasy within a fantasy?

The group struggles with this idea.

Cameron:	It's fantasy because gorillas aren't supposed to be in a house, so it's a fantasy. (He points out details in the cover illustrations.)
Lisa:	There seems to be two things going on, one with the toy gorilla and one with her dad.

Lisa's explicit instruction to "explain fully because you've read the story and others might not have" and her question, "Who else has read this story and would like to add?" encouraged her students to be explicit or decontextualize their comments. Explicitness in this situation is both necessary and useful. She also reminded students to add any knowledge they have to the conversation, and to support one another's comments.

The group spirit that allowed them to work together to understand what they were reading continued across the year as the following discussion in April demonstrates.

As the children discuss Lucia Gonzales's *The Bossy Gallito*, a selection in their literature book, they look at the illustrations.

Cameron:	They tell us it's a parrot. On page 120 it says, "of his uncle, the parrot." That's how I found out it was the parrot.
Maria:	That's how I knew.
Lisa:	Did anyone know in a different way?
Amarachi:	The border of the page. Look in the corner and you can see the word *parrot*.

Finding Out About New Books by Listening to Friends

The children learned that they could get good ideas for what they wanted to read next by listening to their friends tell about a book they had individually read and enjoyed. They made connections to each other through the books they read and shared. The whole group read the complete Frog and Toad and Henry and Mudge series and Patricia Polacco's books as soon as they heard the first one discussed. Book tips did not come only from positive evaluations, however. When Maria talked about a book she'd decided not to finish, Cameron decided that he'd try it because, despite Maria's difficulty with it, he thought, "It sounds good." As the year progressed, group members gave recommendations to other members as they came to know their individual tastes and preferences. Chris does this during a discussion in April:

Chris: Brett, have you read this [*Coyote Places the Stars* by Harriet Peck Taylor]?

Brett: No.

Chris: I think you'd like this book for two reasons. Well, first I got to ask you a question. You really like jaguars, right? Did you like that [jaguar] story?

Brett: Yeah.

Chris: Well, I think you would like it because they are similar. (He goes on to elaborate the similarities, and asks Brett if she's read it, but she hasn't.) The main reason I think you'd be interested is that it was made in Colorado. (Brett had visited Colorado that fall.)

The very next day, Chris switches roles from recommending a book to seeking recommendations, responding to Shida's enthusiastic recommendation of the book he read at home the night before with a quick "I got that book!"

Pulling a Theme Together

At the end of the first theme, Lisa piled all the trade books they had read together and asked the children to sort or organize them in some way. The results were fascinating, giving Lisa a glimpse of how the children organized their experiences.

Books are spread across several desktops, and the children are gathered around them.

Lisa: These are all books that we've shared together and that we've talked about. These are all really good stories. Are there any ways that we could group these books together?

Lisa puts out a group of various buttons and demonstrates how one might group buttons according to different criteria.

Lisa: I have a lot of buttons. There are many different ways to group them.

Students name various ways to group the buttons including color, shape, and texture.

Lisa: Yes, there's no right or wrong. Just many different ways. I want you to work together to talk about how to group the books. No right or wrong. However, if you make a suggestion, you have to have a reason that goes back to the story. You guys have to talk to each other. You're going to come up with a system.

Sarah: *Pink and Say*, *Faithful Friends* (by Robert San Souci), *Matthew and Tilly* (by Rebecca Jones). They all have blacks and they all have whites [people], and they're all friends. And also have dark colors in illustrations.

Lisa: What do you think?

There is no response and so Lisa gives the group some think time before posing another question.

Lisa: Does everyone agree?

Everyone: Yes!

Now, Cameron is willing to try a grouping of a different sort.

Cameron: *Chester's Way* (by Kevin Henkes); *My Painted House, My Friendly Chicken, and Me* by (Maya Angelou); and *Sam, Bangs, and Moonshine* (by Evaline Ness) all have animals in them. *Frog and Toad Are Friends* (by Arnold Lobel), too.

Will: Except *Frog and Toad* have those thingies. I don't know what kind of animals they are.

Lisa: So what are we going to do? Are we going to agree with Cameron?

Will: With Chris?

Lisa:	He hasn't said anything yet. How can we know if we agree with each other or not if we haven't talked?

Lisa is teaching the students to listen, reflect, and take action on the recommendations of peers. She will not let them move on until they make a decision about Cameron's suggestion.

Sarah:	This is really hard.
Maria:	*Grandfather's Journey* (by Allen Say) and *The Faithful Friends* because they are both far away from Athens [Georgia].
Pilar:	*A Birthday Basket for Tia* (by Pat Mora) with *Little Nino's Pizzeria* (by Karen Barbour). Yeah, because they are both in the literature book. No, because they both involve food.
Jasmyn:	Some of the books have people in them, some animals.
Sarah:	Some people and some animals.

The students work hard at drawing generalizations as they attempt to categorize the theme's set of books.

Lisa draws the group close to the pile of books and recaps the groupings suggested by the students. Someone suggests adding *Grandfather's Journey* and *The Faithful Friend* because they involve different races, and they involve taking a trip. Jasmyn agrees that *The Faithful Friend* also has a journey. *Grandfather's Journey* is taken out of the race group and put in the travel story group. Cameron and Jasmyn add *Frog and Toad Are Friends* because the story "The Letter" is in their literature book.

Their decision to place "The Letter" in a category because it appears in the literature book shows the struggle these students had in moving beyond surface details to more abstract categorizations. Lisa allows the students to offer other ways of categorizing. She resists the tendency to jump in and offer a seemingly right answer. In the following dialogue, Lisa has become adept at pulling all students into the discussion. She wants each member of the group to do their own thinking and to share with the group.

Shida:	*Chester's Way* and *Frog and Toad* go together because both have animals as people.
Lisa:	Amarachi, what do you think? Cheng, how about you?

Cheng suggests putting the books in rows. (Perhaps he is reaching for a contribution to this intense conversation. Lisa reiterates the task of grouping books, hoping that Cheng will realize the purpose of the activity.)

Lisa: Should *My Painted House, My Friendly Chicken, and Me* be with black and white books?

Sarah: Yes, but they're not friends.

Lisa suggests that the group try to link all the books together in some way. Cheng continues to insist that they be put in rows, while others continue to interject possibilities. Maria and Sarah quibble over grouping books as having people or not having people.

Cheng: You could go in every single direction from each story.

Lisa: So we're seeing lots of different connections between books. Yeah!

Students again shift books from pile to pile based on different content such as food and people. Lisa stops the group.

Lisa: Let's look at what we have. Take a moment to think. Look at the titles, think about how they're connected, see if we're happy with this. Look at what we've done and think about how all of the books we've read are connected.

Lisa and the students look at the piles of books discussing the groupings one final time. Lisa reiterates the importance of listening to each other and going back to the story.

Lisa: It's not just what you think, but what the story says, too.

In this case, adding trade books to the basal selections not only provided the students with more reading material, it also provided them with a chance to think about connections and to articulate those connections. It offered Lisa the opportunity to hear a little of what and how her students were thinking as they connected one book to another. It also allowed her to again place responsibility and decision making on her students. She made them defend their positions and provide reasons for their suggested groupings. In addition, she encouraged them to articulate their emergent reasoning. Finally, it afforded yet another opportunity to learn how to be an effective member of a group.

Of course other kinds of learning occurred as well. As the children grew as readers and responders, Lisa introduced brief novels as whole-class reading. She read aloud most of the first novel, *Arthur, for the Very*

First Time, with each child reading along in his or her individual copy of the book. When they read *Sarah, Plain and Tall* after winter break, they alternated between Lisa reading chapters aloud as the students read along, and reading chapters on their own at home. Toward the end of the year, as they read *The Whipping Boy*, the children read most chapters at home. Their experiences with a more complex form of novel provided them with opportunities for extended discourse about memorable books, and practice in comprehending longer texts. We'll look at these opportunities in more detail in the next two chapters.

At the end of each theme, the children were united by common experiences with literature that they could carry with them into the next theme. They were also enriched by individual experiences with literature that fed their growing understandings about books. These experiences were possible because of the choices Lisa made as she added to the material present in the basal series. They were, in fact, the foundation for all that occurred in this literature group throughout the year. Because the books were engaging, because they were worth reading and interesting enough to talk about, the literature group had an intrinsic reason for existing.

Reflection Point

Before you begin the next chapter, list in your journal the ways in which you use literature in your classroom. Think about your daily routines. How often do you read aloud? Why do you read aloud? Is reading aloud an integral part of your instructional strategy or merely a pleasant interlude?

Chapter 3

Helping Students Learn About Literature

It's April and Lisa has just shared Amarachi's comment with the group about looking through the faraway end. They have been thinking and talking about Arthur, for the Very First Time off and on since January when Lee read it to them for a second time.

Lisa: Can we apply this to Arthur and his life? Think about him, his struggles, his changes.

The group is quiet, thinking.

Chris: He actually did change to look at the big picture of his life.

Lisa: It's like if you look through the small end, you tend to focus in on one thing. Was Arthur focused on one thing?

Brett: At the beginning he was focused on one thing.

Chris: The baby. But all through the story he was thinking about that.

The group discusses perspective, and Lisa mentions that "sometimes authors do this. You have something concrete like a telescope, but it means more. Uncle Wrisby was telling him to look at his life in a different way." Chris remarks that he thinks about this book frequently. Then Amarachi talks about her moment of epiphany and Chris follows.

Chris: Sometimes when you think something really neat about a story you can't remember it. Amarachi is lucky.

The group talks about remembering.

Lisa: Some books do that. Not all books stick with us.

Chris: Possibly some books are better than others and some books you read more deeply. Like we read. We really get deeply into a story. We read about what happened, and think about

why it happened. We read more deeply than people I know.
They'd say that's cool that happened. We think why did that
happen, who made it happen, and all of that other stuff.
Any question we could think of, we ask.

Lisa asks what reading is, and various students reply.

Brett: *You can become brilliant. My grandma, she reads a lot and*
she's brilliant.

Chris: *I think it depends on what kind of book. If you read a book*
like Arthur, for the Very First Time, *you kind of understand*
life better. If you read a book about weather, you get smarter.

Lisa: *Do you agree there's two kinds of books? Some books teach*
us about life, others help us learn?

The group continues to discuss what books can do.

The connections that students made as they read, wrote, and talked about the books they were offered not only helped them learn how to think and talk about life but also about literature. Their experiences also helped them to learn about literature as an art form. It was no accident that the children referred to their basal as their "literature book," for Lisa treated it as such. Working from the basal, she developed thematic studies with the many additional trade books she brought in for the students to take home to read. Her students participated in author studies and genre studies. They listened to her read aloud, read aloud and silently alone and with a partner, and read chapter books in the group and on their own. They studied literary elements such as character, setting, and style. They also learned to link the books they were reading to books they had read previously and to their own lives, making these important intertextual connections both individually and collaboratively.

Reflection Point

Think about what you would like to teach your students about literature. Jot down your ideas in your journal. As you read this chapter, add ideas that you hadn't thought of.

Learning About the Author's Craft, or How Did This Book Get Here?

Children aren't born knowing that real people write books. For all they know books spring fully formed from the library shelves. As children discuss the books they read, they begin to consider the author's craft, discussing issues of organization, style, and other author decisions. They begin to understand what characterizes a particular writer or illustrator. This, in turn, informs their perceptions of themselves as writers (Graves, 1983).

In March, Lisa and her students discuss Patricia MacLachlan, an author with whom they have become familiar through reading three of her brief novels and several picture books.

Cameron: And I think I know why she always puts, like she makes prairies or barns.

Lisa: Who are you talking about?

Cameron: Patricia MacLachlan. Because if you look on the back of the book in "Something about Patricia MacLachlan," it says that she likes prairie dogs.

Sarah: This [*Skylark*] reminds me of *All the Places to Love* (by Patricia MacLachlan).

Will: Things You Know First [*What You Know First* by Patricia MacLachlan].

Lisa: Both.

Shida: Remember, Papa was putting dirt in his pocket.

At the request of the group, Lisa looks through *What You Know First* and Lee looks through *All the Places to Love*. They both show dirt being put in a pocket. They show the illustrations to the group.

Cameron: In her real life, she carries that dirt.

Lisa: How does it tie to *Skylark*?

Sarah: It's by the same author.

Lisa: Remember how Caleb writes Sarah's name in the dirt? Seems to me that since she carries it around in her pocket and it's in her books, it seems like her name is written in the dirt.

The group discusses whether or not MacLachlan was born on the prairie.

Lisa: That's why I made the connection. You can see in her own writing that she brings very much of herself.

Lisa's book choices allowed students to build on their concepts of author. She read aloud three Patricia MacLachlan novels for students to compare, and made available several of the author's picture books, which initiated a discussion about why the author chose not to use chapter titles in a book. Discussing issues such as this teaches students that writing a book, much like teaching, is a deliberate, planned activity, often drawn from the life and interests of the author. The students responded with letters to the author (see Figure 1 on pages 60–61), which demonstrated their enthusiasm.

Reflection Point

Author studies often become simply compiling several books by a particular author and reading them as a group. However, author studies can be an opportunity for students to learn to compare and contrast, to make connections among books, to make generalizations about an author, to study the relationship between an author's life and his or her work, and to explore style. Think about one of your favorite authors; gather several of that author's books and as much biographical information as you can find. Then sit with the books and jot notes about the connections, comparisons, and generalizations that your students might make after reading and studying the books. Design activities that will help them do this.

Learning Genre Characteristics and Conventions

As students read widely and across genres, they begin to discover the characteristics and conventions that distinguish the genres. This knowledge helps them to understand books they are reading: If you know how a genre

Figure 1
Letters to Patricia MacLachlan

March 17, 1998

Dear Patricia MacLachlan
      Do you have any
children? I thought you
might need someone to
get ideas from, like when Arthur and
Moira got drunk. In "Sarah plain and
tall" and "Skylark" Why didn't you write
names for the chapter but you did
in "Arthur for the very first time"? Are you
very famous? Like do you go to schools?
if you do, could you come to ours?

                Yours truly,
                Chris

      P.S. Do you read your own books?

March 16, 1998

Dear Patricia,
      Do you like kids? Because
we've read many of your books and
most of them contain one or two
children. I love your books. The first one
we ever read was Arthur for the very
first time. Why do you carry a bag of
prairie dirt where ever you go?
Please write more books.

                Love,
                Amarachi Anukam

Figure 1
Letters to Patricia MacLachlan (continued)

March 16, 1998

Dear Ms. Maclachlan,

I have enjoyed your books. By the way my name is /Sarah Weber. / Close to the end of the book Skylark I was very happy, because, the drought was over. In the beginning of Skylark I was sad, because the drought started. I am even worried about Sarah haveing a baby. If you were a reader would you worried! I love the way you describe things.

Love,

Sarah Weber

3-16-98

Dear Patricia Machlan
Why did you make chapter titles in Authur for the very first time and not in Sarah, plain and tall or Skylark? I like how you describ things. I have read alot of your books. I like three names alot. Because of the words and the pictures. My favorite character is three names becase I like dogs. I have three dogs. Two dalmations one Chawawa. The boy dalmation is Lucky the girl one is Freckles the boy chawawa is Peewee.

Maria

works, what the "rules" are, you're more likely to understand and appreciate works within that genre. It also allows students to compare and contrast their reading material, forming important generalizations about the way literature is organized. This organizational ability is especially important for early elementary students as they work together to understand their world. Lisa planned her book selection to cover several genres.

Fantasy and Realism

In Chapter 2, Achala stated with certainty that she knew that *Catwings* was not a true story because cats do not have wings. In the following discussions, Lisa and her students tackle the difficult questions of fiction and nonfiction, and fantasy and realism.

It is early December, and the group has just begun a new theme, Stretch Your Imagination. On the second day of the theme study, Achala offers her *Catwings* comment. The discussion of fantasy and reality continues over the next 2 days.

Lisa has just finished reading "The Green Ribbon" from *In a Dark, Dark Room* (by Alvin Schwartz) and she asks, "Does this story fit into this theme?"

Chris:	It's scary.
Pilar:	Magic.
Lisa:	There is an element of magic, humor. Fantasy can contain an element of humor. When the story starts is it believable?
Cheng:	Yes.
Lisa:	You see how we start in reality and how we are slowly drawn into fantasy.

They continue to discuss other books that students have read individually.

Chris:	*The Z Was Zapped* (by Chris Van Allsburg). To start with, I don't really know why this fits into the theme. It had no characters. Mostly bad things happened to the letters. There was humor.
Jasmyn:	Imaginary events. Really, the letters wouldn't get hurt.
Lisa:	Remember, fantasy is fiction and it twists or manipulates reality. Chris Van Allsburg is a master of it.

The students discuss other books that he has written.

The next day the students continue to share, beginning with two Van Allsburg books.

Jasmyn:	*The Stranger* reminds me of *The Sweetest Fig*.
Lisa:	How?
Brett:	They are both fantasy.
Cheng:	They have to be alike because all fantasies have magic.
Students:	Not necessarily.
Chris:	Julius [*Julius, the Baby of the World* by Kevin Henkes] didn't have magic.
Lisa:	Magic, imaginary characters, and imaginary events might be in fantasy, but don't have to be. Remember how Chris Van Allsburg walks the fine line between what might happen and what is fantasy.

Lisa summarizes the conversation and makes a final comment.

Lisa:	Good thinking! So you see how the author walks that fine line. Some things are believable and some are not.

As the students continue with this theme, they discuss and form generalizations about the elements of fantasy. In January Lisa summarizes what they discovered through their reading and their own writing. She asks them, "Have you read *Where the Wild Things Are* (by Maurice Sendak)? I want to look at it with a new hat on, with new eyes." The students discuss fantasy, generating attributes: fast action, magical events, animals taking on human characteristics, imaginary events, and humor. As Lisa reads the book, Jasmyn remarks that it relates to *Ben's Dream* (by Chris Van Allsburg), and Lisa asks her to "Hold that link." After the story is read, Jasmyn continues:

Jasmyn:	This book relates to *Ben's Dream*.
Lisa:	How?
Jasmyn:	Because in bed after he fell asleep he was having a dream, and there was a lot of pages without words. And in this book, too.

Lisa continues their discussion about whether or not this story contains a dream, then shows them the page where the forest begins to grow and says, "That's where it starts."

Jasmyn:	That's where the fantasy starts.
Lisa:	(flipping back to the page where Max is in his bedroom) This is not fantasy. Maurice Sendak starts out in reality and goes to fantasy.
Brett:	People imagine things.

Lisa ends the theme study with a group discussion of the short novel they have read, *The Celery Stalks at Midnight* by James Howe.

Complicating the Genres: Fiction and Nonfiction

The next theme in the basal, Life Long Ago, centers on dinosaurs but Lisa, delighted with her students' interest in fantasy and their attempts to distinguish it from realistic fiction, decided to expand on this theme. She changed it to Historical Fiction/Historical Nonfiction, hoping to continue the genre discussions. She also planned to build student interest in Patricia MacLachlan by reading *Sarah, Plain and Tall* and *Skylark* before the 6-week study was over. Her plans incorporated the basal theme that she had agreed to follow, allowed her to continue helping her students to explore their interests (genre conventions), and allowed her to encourage her students' delight in Patricia MacLachlan as an author. Fortunately, the basal contained the same mix of nonfiction and fantasy as in the new theme, so the selections supported Lisa's goal.

The theme begins with a reading of *Time Train* (by Paul Fleischman). Lisa reads the story aloud as students follow along. They are immediately pulled into the book, and when they finish, they pronounce it a "good story!"

Lisa:	How many of you would want to be on that time train?
	Every hand goes up.
Sarah:	It would be really cool to see real dinosaurs because then you could write about them.
Jasmyn:	I would have gotten back on the train!
Lisa:	You wouldn't be afraid of the danger?
Cameron:	If Tyrannosaurus rex had come into the story, you can just imagine!
Lisa:	What kind of story is this?
Students:	Fantasy.

Sarah:	Dinosaurs aren't alive.
Brett:	They are extinct.
Lisa:	So, it's not true. Some of the stories we read will be fantasy, some nonfiction, some historical fiction.
Cameron:	Will there be any realistic fiction?

In this discussion, Cameron, the master of intertextual connections, has remembered the discussion of *Arthur, for the Very First Time*. He is also thinking of realistic fiction as being contemporary but not historical.

As they continued with the theme, the students read many books about dinosaurs and other ancient beasts that Lisa brought for independent reading. Some books are nonfiction, some are fantasy, and some are an interesting hybrid in which the fictional story line incorporates a lot of factual information—narrative nonfiction. These books prompted interesting discussions about the information embedded in the fictional story. At first, the children had to decide how the texts work, what is fact and what is fiction, and how to distinguish between the two as they did in this discussion in early February.

Cameron shared *The Littlest Dinosaurs* (by Bernard Most) with the group, and he remarked that he wondered how the egg-stealing dinosaurs got the eggs from the nest. He speculated that they must either jump or fly. Maria told him that the nests are on the ground (fact), and Shida offered, "I think Cameron must be thinking about bird nests, because bird nests are high." Lisa helped him articulate that "dinosaur nests would be kind of low." The children then turn to the illustrations and wonder aloud why a dinosaur is looking in the refrigerator, agreeing that this is not fact but fiction. Cameron then reminded them that "it didn't say that they know he stole, but that scientists think he stole eggs from other dinosaurs," which added another dimension to the discussion. This prompted a discussion of the theories of dinosaur extinction, with the children offering their opinions and Will reminding them that "No one knows how they died for sure. They have all sorts of theories." Jasmyn, seeking closure, asked if the dinosaur dictionary, which they had been consulting as the final authority, has anything in it about extinction.

As the children read within this theme, they brought their sometimes considerable knowledge to the discussions, for instance what they knew about pterodactyals. Their contributions to the conversations were often based on what they knew rather than what they felt or thought, which characterized most of their conversations about fiction. While they tried to distinguish between fiction and nonfiction, they compared sources when discrepancies in information appeared, and began to make distinctions between facts (or what we know) and theory (or what scientists think happened). A look at several books by Aliki prompted discussion about the way she provides information through running text and speech balloons. Students also made links between this theme and a piece in the earlier Nature Spy theme.

By the end of February, they have finished the basal selections and have read many related trade books, and Lisa is ready to introduce another kind of Life Long Ago book—historical fiction. She begins by talking to the group about fiction.

Lisa:	What do you know about fiction?
Jasmyn:	It's not real.
Lisa:	What about *Arthur, for the Very First Time*?
Sarah:	Nonfiction.
Chris and Will:	No! Realistic fiction.

Students talk about animals understanding people. Lisa asks what is not real. Sarah and Jasmyn continue to insist that it's nonfiction.

Chris:	It could have been real. She just made it up. It didn't actually happen, but it could have.
Lisa:	That's why we call it realistic.

The group goes on to discuss Arthur and Wrisby, real and not real. Lisa summarizes.

Lisa:	*Arthur, for the Very First Time* is what we call realistic fiction. It was a made-up story, but everything in it actually could have happened.

Discussion ensues and Lisa once again summarizes.

Lisa:	So the author might start with things that they're familiar with, with their own life, and then add to that things that they made up. We're going to continue with Patricia MacLachlan as an author, but move to historical fiction, *Sarah, Plain and Tall*. There are characters, setting, plot,

but long ago. It's not about dinosaurs but about settling the west. MacLachlan did some research about how characters dressed, talked, and thought. It's a made-up story, but it could have happened.

They go on to discuss how the character of Arthur changed in the story and how they'll look for other characters changing in the present story.

Lisa: As the plot developed in the story, the character was changing. So those are the same things we'll look for in *Sarah, Plain and Tall*. We'll look for the characters to change as the story goes on. So, historical fiction is grounded in facts. Authors do research about what life was like, types of food, clothes, and animals, because it has to be realistic.

As you can see from these discussions, students learned about literature by actively thinking about and discussing what they had read, and responding to Lisa's probing questions as well as her brief lectures about the genres. This continued as the year progressed, with each new reading experience adding to what the students knew about genre characteristics (see Box 3-2).

BOX 3-2
Genres and Their Characteristics

PICTURE BOOKS: Story or concept presented through a combination of text and illustration. Interdependence of art and text. Classification based on format, not content. All other genres appear in picture book format.

POETRY AND VERSE: Condensed language, imagery. Distilled, rhythmic expression of imaginative thoughts and perceptions.

FOLKLORE: Traditional stories, myths, legends, nursery rhymes, and songs from the oral tradition. No known author.

FANTASY: Stories set in places that do not exist, about people and creatures that could not exist, or events that could not happen. Imaginative worlds, make-believe.

SCIENCE FICTION: Stories about what might occur in the future based on extending physical laws and scientific principles to their logical outcomes.

CONTEMPORARY REALISTIC FICTION: Stories that could happen in today's real world.

HISTORICAL FICTION: Stories that could have happened that are set in the past.

BIOGRAPHY: Stories about the life or part of the life of a real human being.

NONFICTION: Texts that present facts about the real world, or that explain a subject or concept.

From Cullinan, B.E., & Galda, L. (1998). *Literature and the child* (4th ed.). Fort Worth, TX: Harcourt Brace.

Learning How Stories Work

Most of the books Lisa added to the basal themes were stories—narratives—that supported the theme in some way. Even in the themes Nature at Your Door and Life Long Ago, in which the focus was mainly on dinosaurs, Lisa selected fiction for reading aloud. For example, Nature Spy presented the opportunity to read aloud together *Arthur, for the Very First Time*, and Life Long Ago evolved into an opportunity to read *Sarah, Plain and Tall* and *Skylark*. It is clear from the previous discussions that Lisa's students did much more than read. In her classroom, reading and discussing a story was always an opportunity to discover more about how stories work. Over the year, Lisa's students discussed setting, style, plot, theme, illustrations, and character development.

Learning About Setting

By incorporating historical fiction into the book selections, Lisa ensured that her students would talk about setting, which is an important element in historical fiction. Children often notice setting simply because the details of life are different. Much of the following discussion came about as the students talked about Patricia MacLachlan as an author. At the end of February, the group is talking about MacLachlan liking animals because her stories contain farms.

Will:	People who love the land.
Brett:	That's maybe like she is. Maybe she lives on a farm. The books we've read so far have been set on a farm.
Lisa:	I'll share more Patricia MacLachlan books with you and that would be a good thing to look for.

Later, they return to the topic of setting, discussing what they have noticed about most of Patricia MacLachlan's books (dogs, chickens, and horses).

Jasmyn:	In some of them the setting might be old days.
Cameron:	I agree.
Brett:	Maybe she likes to write about the past.
Will:	*Arthur, for the Very First Time* was now, but *Sarah, Plain and Tall*, *Three Names*, and *All the Places to Love* were a long time ago.

In discussions of setting, students paid careful attention to illustrations especially if they were reading picture books. As they read, thought, wrote, and talked, students asked about setting when it was important to their understandings of the text.

Learning About Style

With a large poster proudly proclaiming Word Wonderment, Lisa constantly drew her students' attention to the words authors used. She demonstrated how she noticed especially interesting words and phrases as she read, and she asked students to bring words to the group for discussion. This served several functions: It allowed her to help students notice the language that an author used, it became the basis of vocabulary instruction, and it provided opportunities to discuss word-attack skills. (The latter two functions are discussed in Chapter 4.)

These practices evolved from discussions throughout the year. For example, in mid-September the group shares books they read the night before. Sarah, who read *Grandfather's Journey*, asks about the word *astonished*:

Lisa:	Astonished. What a wonderful word. We can write it down in our journals. Can we think of strategies to figure out what it means? Can we figure out what it means?

The group offers *surprised* and *amazed*.

Lisa:	Yes. He'd never seen anything like it before.
Cheng:	I've seen the ocean before.
Lisa:	Yes, but he didn't. Can you imagine the first time you see it!

Lisa goes on to talk about context clues, using the glossary in the back of the basal and a dictionary, and how students need only to know the gist of the word as they read unless they can't guess the meaning. Later, she'll ask students to write down words that they have noticed in their reading, find their definitions, and share them with the class for inclusion on the Word Wonderment wall.

Learning about style didn't stop with enjoying individual words and phrases. In a November discussion of *Arthur, for the Very First Time*, the group grapples with a difficult metaphor that MacLachlan incorporates.

Jasmyn:	When it first started, the house was a book.

Pilar:	On the back it said that.
Lisa:	What does that mean? Patricia MacLachlan does that a lot.
Cameron:	The house is a book. Wrisby and Elda are the characters.
Lisa:	What does that mean? Think about your book. Ponder that a little. You open a book...
Jasmyn:	It starts making sounds. Opening a book is like opening a door to a house.
Lisa:	What happens?
Cameron:	We are turning into characters. We are imagining that we are in the book.
Pilar:	We just float around in a tornado and know we are in the book.
Lisa:	So that house, when he is on the outside, is like an ordinary house. Arthur is becoming part of that story when he goes inside.

And, as you remember, this is the book that gave rise to Amarachi's insight about viewpoints and visions.

The consideration of style carried across the year, especially when the group discussed authors they knew well, like Patricia MacLachlan.

Learning About Plot

Often, discussion of plot was intertwined with that of the events of the story as children worked to make sense of what they had read. Especially at the beginning of the year, Lisa encouraged children to return to the text and to help each other as they talked. This focus on knowing what happened, to whom, and in what order helped the group to make the transition from short picture books to longer fiction. Keeping track of what happened and when ensured that they all understood the sense of the story. Sometimes, the complexity of the stories made understanding the events especially demanding, as seen in the following December discussion of Van Allsburg's *The Stranger*.

Lisa asks if the stranger, who had amnesia, ever figured out who he was. Will and Chris think that he did, but no one else agrees. Lisa asks what clues made them think that. They go on to discuss picking up rabbits and blowing on a leaf, exploring the illustrations that depict these events. Lisa summarizes.

> **Lisa:** Let's look at clues in the story. He blows on the leaves, then he comes to dinner dressed in his leather, and then he is ready to leave. Does he want to have green leaves? What did he do?

The group then discusses why leaves change color, how the stranger's body temperature was very low when he first arrived, and how the rabbits were not afraid of him. Someone offers the interpretation that the stranger might have been an alien.

> **Lisa:** It could be an alien, but you have to ask if it fits with the story.

After a brief discussion, they reluctantly conclude that the alien explanation does not fit the story. The discussion continues.

> **Sarah:** Most of these things could really happen, but a few of them could not.
>
> **Lisa:** What?
>
> **Sarah:** Blowing on a leaf.
>
> **Will:** Low body temperature.
>
> **Brett:** Maybe he went out on the road because he was looking for something else to do; maybe he wanted to visit another place.
>
> **Chris:** Maybe he was going from west to east, looking for places that were green so that he could turn them orange.
>
> **Cameron:** Yeah, you're right. He's like some kind of magical god, and he is changing the weather.

This was a complicated story with much left to inference, and the children had to struggle with putting the events together into a meaningful, centered whole before they could begin to understand them.

Reflection Point

Write in your journal about why you read. What makes you spend time with a good story, a poem, or a nonfiction text?

Exploring Themes

An exploration of themes in the selections the children read was easy because their reading experiences were organized around themes. From the beginning, Lisa reminded them that the books were connected because each explored the same general theme, as seen in the preceeding excerpts. In September, she reminds them of this as they work in pairs to discuss *Little Nino's Pizzeria*:

Lisa: Okay, great. But remember there are other things (besides favorite parts) you can think about. Not only can you talk about your favorite part, but also what you learned about families. Open your literature book to the story and talk about what you learned about families. By tomorrow I want you to have thought about the story enough to talk about the ideas in the story. Open the book and look at it as you talk. If you're talking about the illustrations, you should be looking at them. These are very important things for you to be thinking about. We've moved on to the second part of our theme, families. So we need to be thinking about families. What did you learn about families? Is this family different from your family? It's different from my family. So you might want to discuss this with your partners.

A focus on theme was still present at the end of the year. In the following discussion, students have been talking about *The Whipping Boy*, which they have just finished. After summarizing the students' discussion, Lisa asks:

Lisa: What did this book teach us about life? I don't think Sid Fleischman's purpose was to tell us about life in the sewers. As readers we have to link everything together. We have to think about the big idea.

Chris: Well, I kind of think it was about friends and stuff. We kind of agreed about that. Prince Brat left, ran away with Jemmy to see if he could find a friend.

Cameron: So he wouldn't get lost.

Lisa: Wait. You are getting to a little idea. Stay with the big idea. We are looking through the faraway end. If Sid Fleischman writes about friendship, what did you learn?

Do you agree? Is there one thing you might learn about friendship that you might apply to your own life? Can you apply it to your life?

The group continues to discuss the big ideas in the novel, and Lisa summarizes:

Lisa: You are saying the big ideas are friendship and loneliness. You see throughout the story that Jemmy had some revelations about Prince Brat. No love. Remember, that's another theme you found—love and care.

Although it was difficult for some students to look through the far-away end, the regularity with which Lisa related each book to the theme they were exploring, the connections she encouraged them to make between books and across themes, and the links she encouraged them to make between their reading and their lives were clear demonstrations of how to read and think about books. By encouraging them to make these intertextual connections Lisa offered her students the opportunity to use books to understand literature and life.

Exploring Illustrations

Not surprisingly, these young readers were used to exploring illustrations, and did so regularly to help them build meaning as they read and discussed. Even while reading chapter books, they made use of the limited illustrations, thoroughly savoring and analyzing each picture.

In late September they are discussing *The Table Where Rich People Sit* (illustrated by Peter Parnall), and Cameron uses the illustrations to query Sarah about a comment she made.

Sarah: She wants to have pretty dresses and go to pretty places.

Cameron: But they were, like, in the middle of the desert!

Lisa: How do you know they are in the desert?

Cameron: Because everything looks so hot and stuff.

Later, Lisa introduces a discussion of the distinctive use of line, space, and color in Peter Parnall's illustrations.

The next day, Shida comments that Mudge's eyes in *Henry and Mudge Get the Cold Shivers* (by Cynthia Rylant) look "weird."

Lisa:	What's "weird" mean? I like weird things.
Shida:	His eyes look different.
Lisa:	Why do you think the illustrator did that?
Students:	Because she wanted Mudge to look sick.

The group then discusses what a good artist Shida is and how he notices details in illustrations.

Repeatedly, Lisa praised students for noticing things in the illustrations. She pointed out details in illustrations and asked students to look at illustrations while they tried to understand what they were reading.

When the group reads *Arthur, for the Very First Time*, their first novel, Sarah comments on her fondness for picture books:

Sarah:	I feel like I need a break.
Lisa:	What does that mean?
Sarah:	I wouldn't want to read chapter books all my life. I like seeing pictures.

Indeed, the move from picture books to chapter books is a big move for young readers. No longer holding a large, familiar 32-page book in their hands, with pictures to help with textual meaning, these second graders were relying entirely on print to create meaning. Although students were reading novels as a group, picture-book reading also was available in the literature books and in the books they checked out for reading at home.

Some books such as Chris Van Allsburg's *The Z Was Zapped* demand attention to the illustrations, especially because there is very little text. Sarah has brought this book to the group and begins with a comment on the illustrations:

Sarah:	I wonder about the first picture. I'd hate to be underneath the stage, straight down. You'd have problems, like you'd smell the dog breath.
Lisa:	So when you say that are you imagining what it would be like to be there with different letters?
Sarah:	Yes. I'd love to be there under the *I* for *ice cream*!

Jasmyn comments on the illustrations and Sarah adds, "It looks like someone is holding the letters down."

Later, when the group discussed Mark Teague's *Pigsty,* and Cameron was puzzled by what the pigs in the book are doing. Lisa reminded him that it is fantasy and asked if the pigs are taking on human characteristics. Immediately the children intently focused on the illustrations, discussing the real and fantastic details within them. The group continued to discuss several other books, always exploring the illustrations. Sarah opened a brief discussion of perspective (word supplied by Lisa) and how that changes what we see in illustrations.

This pattern of looking at illustrations to understand meaning continued even when the group read *The Whipping Boy* in the spring. At times it seemed that their close scrutiny of the illustrations in the chapter openings got in the way of their thinking about the story. But not wanting them to abandon a very important meaning-making strategy, Lisa allowed them the freedom to talk about the illustrations and how they reflect the contents of the chapters. One focus of the group was on how the characters are visually portrayed on the cover and in the sketches that occasionally appeared in some of the chapter books they read.

Reflection Point

For interesting explorations of what children notice and understand as they look at illustrations in picture books, read "Individual Literary Response Styles of Young Children" (Sipe, 1998) or *The Potential of Picture Books: From Visual Literacy to Aesthetic Understanding* (Kiefer, 1994). The following books and articles can increase your own understandings about how picture books work: *Wings of an Artist: Children's Book Illustrators Talk About Their Art* (Keifer, 1999); *Words About Pictures: The Narrative Art of Children's Picture Books* (Nodelman, 1990); and "How Picture Books Work: A Semiotically Framed Theory of Text-Picture Relationships (Sipe, 1998).

Focusing on Character Development

One feature of the books Lisa selected was the presence of memorable characters. This was not accidental, for good stories generally do have memorable characters, and because Lisa planned to explore character and character development with her students. In the class discussions presented earlier, Lisa referred to characters growing and changing, a focus that began early in the school year.

In the second week of September, the students are sharing books they have read individually. Cameron has just shared John Peterson's *The Littles*, and he comments that the characters are very small. Lisa asks them to think a little more about the stories they are reading.

> Lisa: Can you think of how your book relates to other books? Have you thought about how the characters change in the book? Let's go beyond "my favorite page."

They then disperse to finish their letters to Toad (they have all read a "Frog and Toad" story in the literature book), focusing on ways to make him feel better.

A week later Achala talks about *Henry and Mudge and the Careful Cousin*:

> Achala: I noticed that Annie was really quiet, just like me. It's a changing story.
>
> Lisa: What changes?
>
> Achala: Annie.
>
> Lisa: I liked how you didn't just say your favorite page but talked about a character and the character's changing in the story.

The comments about character slowly but surely developed into more extended discussions. Sometimes the discussions began with a student wondering about what a character felt, said, or did, as in the following October discussion of *Arthur, for the Very First Time*:

> Cheng: Why would they like strawberries? I mean, I don't like them. I mean my whole family likes them. My dad likes it, my mom likes it. I don't know why. I don't like sour things. And they don't like sour things. I don't know about that.

Lisa: Let's stop there, Cheng. Let's give people a chance to respond. You brought up a lot of "don't knows" and "I wonders." Think about that. Why would he like strawberries?

Brett: 'Cause they're good.

Lisa: Cheng, through this book I hope you're realizing people aren't all the same. That we're different. Arthur's probably a very different person than you are, right? I'm a different person than you are. Achala's different than I am. What Achala likes, I might like some of the same things; sometimes we don't like the same things. And that's okay.

Will: Like my sister loves tomato and I don't like it at all.

Lisa: Exactly. So, are you having trouble understanding why a character would like strawberries?

Cheng: Yeah.

Lisa: Why not? Should all characters in the world be like Cheng?

Cameron: No.

Jasmyn: People are different from each other.

Lisa: That would be boring, wouldn't it?

Cameron: Yes. Because some people are different.

Sarah: Some people are active. People act in different ways.

Cameron: Some people don't like animals; some people do.

Lisa: But by knowing, do you understand, or by Patricia MacLachlan telling us that he does like strawberries and Moira likes strawberries, it helps build a character. It makes them real if we know their likes and dislikes. Do you understand that? That by knowing all those details, he becomes real. With Moreover, we don't know all those details. He is not a main character; he's a flat character. We don't know that much about his personality. So, by knowing all those details about Arthur, I feel I know him really well. Like he's a friend. Authors do that. They give you all that information so you do know them like a friend.

Cameron: It's like Arthur just jumped out of the book!

In this discussion, Lisa took a seemingly off-task comment by Cheng and turned it into a lesson on character development and, concurrently, another lesson on author's craft. Later, she followed up her students' growing interest in the unique characters in this novel by asking them to do character sketches.

*Reflection Point*_____

Take home and reread the stories that you use in your classroom on a regular basis, paying attention to the characters and how they are developed. Write down thumbnail descriptions of the characters and references from the text to support your descriptions. The next time you read these stories with students, begin a discussion about character and see where your students lead you.

_____

As students read and discuss characters, they continue to construct their understanding of characters through their conversations (see Box 3-3 on page 80). Although some scholars suggest that young or pre-adolescent readers are unable to understand character perspective (Beach & Wendler, 1987; Shannon, Kameenui, & Baumann, 1988), the collaborative wisdom of the group and a teacher's careful nudging can create a greater understanding (see the following mid-November discussion). Notice what Lisa teaches her students about how stories work (*Arthur, for the Very First Time*) and about interesting words and group process:

Lisa:	And at the end, when he says, "Why, she looked almost pleasant." Why does he think she looks pleasant?
Cheng:	Because she likes having babies. Oh, yeah, he wouldn't know that.
Will:	It didn't tell us in the book. There's not enough information, really.

Several students agree with Will. Someone suggests looking for clues.

Pilar:	She is clean.
Lisa:	He likes her because she's clean, Pilar?
Cameron:	That doesn't make sense.
Lisa:	You're right, Will. It isn't spelled out for you. It's a gap. You have to go back and figure it out. What experience did he have? What might change his perspective on how the pig looked?

Sarah:	I know.

Sarah: I know.

Lisa: Let's everybody just take 5 seconds and reflect on that.

Sarah: When he first got there, maybe he'd never seen a pig before and they just looked, you know, sometimes pigs look gross the first time you see them. But then, after a while, they don't seem gross. He's been at Uncle Wrisby's farm for a while, and now he actually gets close to her.

Lisa: Ooooh, I like that word *close*, a good descriptive word. Before, he made an impression based on what he had seen from a distance. So now, he's getting close to something. It's a different perspective.

Sarah: Now he's doing things.

Lisa: Yes, he's doing things.

Sarah: He's changing.

Lisa: He's changing.

Chris: Now, he's learning that all the stuff on the outside really doesn't matter. He's learning that she may look ugly, but that doesn't mean she really is ugly on the inside. She's really nice on the inside.

The group continues to explore the concept of character change as they read other stories throughout the year. In May, during a discussion of *The Whipping Boy*, Shida comments on how Prince Brat is changing:

Shida: I think Prince Brat is changing nice.

Sarah: I remember when I said he was changing a little, he was opening a little bit, but now I said a few days ago or yesterday that he's inside out, meaning that he's nice.

Shida: Also, I have something to say about yesterday. Remember yesterday after he got whipped, he changed nice. Maybe the whipping got the bad thing away from him.

Pilar: He's trying to push the bad things away and pull the good thing to him and that's making him want to be like Jemmy because Jemmy's nice.

The students continue to elaborate on Jemmy's role in turning Prince Brat into a nicer person.

BOX 3-3
Techniques for Developing and Revealing Character

Authors let readers know about their characters through the following:

• The way a character looks.

• The way a character acts.

• What a character says and thinks.

• What other characters say about a character.

• The actions other characters take toward a character.

Becoming Sophisticated, Responsive Readers

Over time, the children in this literature group learned to think about different ways to share their thoughts as they read. During the spring, they came up with a list of sharing options (see Box 3-4), which came from their conversations about books throughout the year. By spring, they were quite sophisticated in how they thought and how they talked about their reading.

One way that students learned about literary elements and techniques was by discussing books in relation to other books. They also used their own life experiences to understand or be puzzled by the characters, events, and ideas encountered in the books they read. Linking books to books and to life, or making intertextual links, is a powerful way of learning about literature. We have seen many examples of how Lisa helped her students link books they were reading to other books, to their lives, and to their developing literary knowledge. They also learned to link incidents and feelings within stories to each other, thus promoting greater comprehension, which is discussed in Chapter 4.

BOX 3-4
Ways to Share in Discussions in Literature Group

1. Share responses, prior knowledge, and personal experiences.
2. Discuss feelings about the book.
3. Relate the book to other books, movies, and shows.
4. Ask questions for clarification and interest.
5. Explain and add to your written responses.

In April, the group has a passionate discussion of *The Whipping Boy*:

Pilar: I thought that when Prince Brat had told Cutwater that Jemmy was hiding in bed, I was like, Jemmy, do something. And then if Jemmy didn't do something...

Jasmyn: Just do it for him.

Pilar: Yeah, just do it for him. If I was Jemmy, I'd just do it.

Lisa: You can imagine yourself there and doing something?

Pilar: Yeah.

Cameron: I would distract his.... If I just got sucked into the book, I would start distracting Cutwater and giving Jemmy and Prince Brat time to run away.

Maria: I was really thinking about would Prince Brat go with the plan or would he not? And I thought he would not go with the plan because he didn't want to leave, because before he said he didn't want to leave.

Pilar: Yeah. He just seemed like he didn't want to go.

Lisa: That's interesting, Maria. So you're saying that he's almost thinking it's better to stay where he is than to get this freedom and to have to risk it on the streets or possibly go back to the castle.

Sarah: I think the Prince didn't want to go back.

Chris: I think he [the prince] likes him [Jemmy].

Brett: I think they're gonna be friends.

Cameron: In the inside he likes him, but on the outside he's just mean.

Lisa: Mmmm. What does that mean, Cameron? I understand what you're saying about the inside is different from the outside, but why do you think that is?

Sarah: You can always be good on the inside, but be bad on the outside.

Cameron: Like a good heart, but on the outside there's a bad heart.

Lisa: Why would we only be seeing the outside of him?

Brett: I don't think he likes anyone to know that he likes Jemmy.

Jasmyn: Maybe he just wants people to know that on the outside. Like he likes him on the inside, but he actually doesn't know how to tell everybody he does.

This late-April conversation echoes previous conversations. The group had been talking about perspective and about the possible inconsistency between a character's personality and actions, ever since they first read *Arthur, for the Very First Time* in November. Yet this conversation sounds different from the initial, halting discussions these students had then. Now they are participating; there is a polite but urgent rhythm to the turns, and they're talking about the story and the characters as if they are real. And indeed, they are real to these readers in a very important way. The students have become active, responsive readers who approach stories as potential experiences, and who expect to meet characters they will come to know as friends.

When effective readers read stories, they read for the experience rather than for information they might take away. Louise Rosenblatt (1995) calls this kind of reading "aesthetic" or a "lived-through experience" with the text. This experience is the result of a transaction between the reader as person and the text as words on the page. As words are read, readers evoke a story world that is a combination of all they bring to their reading—experience, knowledge, attitude—and the guidance that the text provides. This evocation is fleeting, ephemeral, existing only in the moment of reading. Aesthetic reading focuses on the evocation or lived-through experience and the feelings, images, ideas, questions, and connections that arise. These individual experiences, brought to the group, form the basis for the exchange of ideas that builds and strengthens each initial response (Galda, 1988). Through interactive discussions, students' understandings are confirmed, enhanced, or questioned (Karolides, 1997).

But what do readers do when they engage in aesthetic reading? Wilhelm (1995) offers a detailed description. He demonstrates how students' responses show that they (1) enter the story world, (2) show interest in the story action, (3) relate to characters, (4) see the story world, (5) elaborate on the story world, (6) connect literature to life, (7) consider the significance of story elements, (8) recognize literary conventions, (9) recognize reading as a transaction, and (10) evaluate the author and themselves as readers.

Many of these dimensions of response have been displayed in the discussions in this book by students recalling in the group what they thought and felt as they read. Often students joyfully entered the story world, talking about what they anticipated from their reading, especially as they learned to make connections across texts. They showed great interest in the story action, peppering their discussions with wonderings, confusions, and support for a character's action. They related to characters, seeking to understand their inside as well as their outside selves. They actively visualized the story world, often speaking of "picturing," "seeing," and "imagining" the characters and events. They elaborated on the story world, often enacting new situations, settings, and episodes. They clearly connected literature to life to both lived experience and experiences with other books. They considered the significance of actions and events in the stories as they worked together to understand those stories. They came to notice and understand literary conventions, how authors used them, and how they worked to shape a story. They understood, through their many discussions, that creating meaning was transactional—that they were part of their own understanding about the stories. And, they grew adept at evaluating the authors and their own performance as readers.

As is most always the case, the whole was greater than the sum of its parts. Talking about the kinds of literary learning that these students engaged in seems to simplify what is actually quite a complex process. The steps in this literary dance are quite intricate, and the rhythms keep changing. Each small piece of newly found understanding enlarged the students' potential as readers. Each book read and discussion enlarged the repertoire of ideas from which they could draw as they read the next book (Cullinan & Galda, 1998). As they were learning about literature, they also were learning about the process of reading and responding to literature. They were learning to be sophisticated, responsive readers.

Reflection Point

Go to the list of ways in which you use literature in your classroom (see Reflection Point on page 55). Now list the things you would like to teach your students about literature. How far apart are your two lists? Write about ways you might change your practice.

Chapter 4

Teaching Reading With Literature: A Focus on Engagement and Comprehension

It's the beginning of March, and the literature group is discussing Sarah, Plain and Tall, *trying to make sense of why Papa and Sarah were arguing in the barn. They've decided that it was "a word fight," and not a "real, punching" fight, clearing up some confusion on the part of Cameron. Sarah brings up a question she has, asking what "crisply" means, which describes the way Sarah is speaking:*

Lisa: *Can you imagine how she might sound? Based on the character of Sarah?*

Discussion ensues.

Lisa: *What I'm saying is that you have to think about how it's being used to describe her words.*

Sarah: *The word sounds happy.*

Cameron: *But she's kind of angry.*

They discuss Sarah's emotions, agreeing that she's angry because she wants to ride a horse and drive the wagon and Papa doesn't want her to. Then Cameron reveals just how involved he is in this story.

Cameron: *If I were Papa, I would say "take it one step at a time."*

Chris: *I would say there is a storm.*

Sarah and Brett: *They didn't know a storm was coming.*

Sarah: *He could say, "Maybe tomorrow."*

Chris: *That's what I am saying.*

Lisa:	Who knew, who knew that tomorrow would be better? Why does Caleb say, "Say no, Papa"?
Brett:	He doesn't want her to leave.
Sarah:	That's what I'm thinking he thought.
Cameron:	I heard when Patricia MacLachlan was making similes, like [saying that] Caleb [was] being [like] a chicken behind her.
Chris:	Yes, that was a simile.

Chris finds another simile, and Cameron leans over to read the very last sentence.

The group discusses the simile, and Jasmyn offers a comparison to Arthur, for the Very First Time, *noting that in both stories the "air grew still" before a storm. They then discuss the emotion in this, and the threat of tornadoes.*

Lisa:	I like what Will said about there being a tornado in their emotions. They are kind of all swirled up.
Chris:	I was thinking that Patricia MacLachlan was trying to make a relationship there. That she was meaning that these two, Sarah and Jacob, when they started arguing maybe she was trying to make it more exciting and scary.
Sarah:	You want to get into the book more. I want to hear the rest.
Brett:	She wanted me to read faster and faster.

isa believes that teachers need to broaden the lens on reading instruction. In the past, schools have focused too narrowly on traditional skills and strategies. In the previous discussion, multiple opportunities for teaching and learning occurred as the literature group talked about books. The group worked together on comprehending an event and meaning within a particular context, understanding an author's style and how it influenced their emotional engagement, and monitoring their own comprehension and reactions to their reading. Every day, Lisa's instruction included strategies and skills such as working with prior knowledge, developing word-identification skills, and strengthening comprehension skills, but also included responding to text, and writing and talking with others to understand text. She also highlighted how to use context clues in sentences, passages, and chapters to infer meaning. All the skills and strategies she taught were embedded in the context of the books they were reading; but she was informed also by her knowledge of how children learn, what they need to know in order to be successful readers, and the requirements of her school and district. Although the basal provided ideas for skill and strategy instruction, Lisa, as a knowledgeable, responsive teacher, rarely followed the teachers' guide, preferring, instead, to rely on her own observations and assessments. Finally, her emphasis on intertextual links strengthened her students' critical thinking skills. The difficult part was doing all of this while also teaching her students about literature and how to discuss books with others.

In Lisa's classroom, reading instruction occurred in tandem with literary instruction, creating a seamless instructional environment for students to learn to read fluently and critically. Reading has been an important part of Lisa's life, and her passion for reading and making sense of literature is evident in her conversations with students. She wants her students not only to be able to read fluently but to enjoy the process of reading and discussing books.

We know from research that the best way to improve reading fluency and comprehension is by reading (Anderson, Hiebert, Scott, & Wilkinson, 1985). Throughout the year Lisa provided students with ample time to practice reading. She also provided a variety of reading opportunities that met the diverse needs of those readers who were on the brink of becoming sophisticated readers. These opportunities included independent reading, paired reading, choral reading, and being read aloud to nearly every day.

These students became independent readers in the same way we all learn a new task—with lots of practice and support. Four days a week, students self-selected books from theme baskets, which they read independently or with family members at home. Lisa made available a wide range of material that supported, challenged, and extended the abilities of her varied students (see Appendix A for lists of these books). After reading, rereading, and discussing these books with peers, students grew more confident in their ability to construct meaning. Discussions of the independently read books as well as of those read in common provided Lisa with the opportunity to observe and assess her students' increasing comprehension, which often sparked an impromptu lesson.

As the group continues their discussion of *Skylark*, Amarachi mentions that she does not understand what it means that the drought was a "mixed blessing," and Lisa uses this as a catalyst for vocabulary and comprehension instruction.

Lisa:	Do you know what it means and why Sarah might have said it?
Jasmyn:	There's two things that she wanted to be blessed with, so it was mixed.
Lisa:	Does everybody understand this? What is the blessing? Jasmyn, what did you mean?
Jasmyn:	Well, she probably meant when she and the family wanted to save water, that she might have wanted to save water and do something else and want to be blessed by something else, so that would be a mixed blessing.
Cameron:	Say that one more time!
Jasmyn:	She wanted to be blessed with two things and it would be mixed.
Cameron:	Let's say she wanted to be blessed with keeping water and washing the floor.
Lisa:	We have to think about what's just happened before that. Let's read that part. (They read.) So, there she is scrubbing the floor. Does she like it? How many of you love your chores? So, Sarah might be happy that she doesn't have to do her chores this week, but on the other hand, she's feeling sad because that means there isn't enough water. Jasmyn, do you understand that?

Not only did students have extensive opportunities for independent reading, they also were expected to read with partners, for example, while reading *Frog and Toad*. During paired reading, Lisa would conduct reading conferences with individual students, which gave her an opportunity to gain important information about their growth as readers. In these conferences, students read aloud to Lisa, and she offered specific ideas regarding word attack, comprehension, and other strategies, as well as ways to begin a literary conversation.

In mid-November, Brett, Amarachi, and Chris are discussing the character of Uncle Wrisby from *Arthur, for the Very First Time*, when Amarachi says, "He is rude." Lisa asks for clarification of the word *rude*, and a discussion ensues:

Lisa: What would you say? How does he say things? Does he say things in a rude manner? What is his relationship with Arthur? Is he rude to Arthur? Think of all the ways that you can communicate. How does he talk to Arthur and how does Arthur talk to him? What kind of relationship do they have?

Brett: They like each other.

Lisa: How?

As the small-group discussion progresses, Lisa leads them to talking about teasing and joking. Chris remarks that Wrisby and Arthur love each other, and Lisa reads aloud a section of dialogue from the book.

Lisa: So, he's kind of a jokester. When he is saying that about Aunt Elda's cooking, it could be a joke.

With that comment, Lisa leaves the group, and they continue their discussion of Uncle Wrisby's character.

During read-aloud time, Lisa often engaged in an oral think-aloud of her own reading processes, helping students see her connections and hesitations as she made meaning.

The group is discussing *Skylark* and Patricia MacLachlan as an author. Cameron remarks that MacLachlan carries dirt around with her in her "real life."

Lisa: Remember how Caleb writes Sarah's name in the dirt? Seems to me that since she carries it around in her pocket and it's in her books, it seems like her name is written in the dirt. That's why I made the connection. You can see in her own writing that she brings very much of herself.

These different kinds of reading and opportunities to talk and listen provided Lisa with critical information about what to teach next, how to nudge students along, and when to suggest alternative strategies. These kinds of teaching opportunities abound when, like Lisa, teachers are knowledgeable about books, children, and what literacy skills children need to develop. This was visible because the children were actively engaged in being connected, responsive readers, focusing on the ideas in the texts they read and the discussions they participated in.

Reading as a Transaction

Reading is active, not passive. Readers construct meaning as they read (Goodman, 1985) rather than acquire it. Personal experiences with life and with other literature, feelings, and purposes all influence the meaning a reader creates while reading a text. This duet between reader and text, often called a transaction because each influences the other (Rosenblatt, 1978), results in the creation of meaning.

The most important aspects of teaching reading to this group were that students were taught (1) to respond to the experiences they were creating as they read stories and poems—or aesthetic response, and (2) to respond to the point being made or ideas presented in nonfiction text—efferent reading. This focus on the approach or stance that readers take toward texts forced Lisa's students to consider their purpose for reading and how purpose, text, and process worked together (Many & Cox, 1992). It also forced the group members to be active and participatory—engaged readers.

Reading From Different Stances

Judith Langer (1995) describes how readers read by (1) being out of and stepping in to a text world—"envisionment"; (2) being in and moving through that envisionment; (3) stepping out and rethinking what one knows about the world; and, finally, (4) stepping out and reconsidering the experience of reading. The difference, Langer argues, between reading from an aesthetic or an efferent stance lies not in the process that readers go through, which remains the same, but in their orientation (stance) to that process. A reader reading from an aesthetic stance would focus on the "horizon of possibilities" that stories and poems provide; a reader reading from an efferent stance would focus on an increasingly convergent point, trying to make sense of or build a concept from the pieces of information presented in the text. Thus active readers respond to texts accordingly, making decisions that affect the meaning that results from reading.

Reading from an aesthetic stance involves being aware of the sound and feeling of a text, as well as identifying with the characters and participating in the story world. It means participating in a virtual rather than an actual experience. This kind of reading gives readers the emotional space in which to evaluate the feelings, actions, and decisions of the story world, and thus to construct their own personal values (Britton, 1970). This kind of reading is potentially transformative. The literature group's many discussions about MacLachlan's novels or Fleischmann's *The Whipping Boy* are full aesthetic responses. Efferent reading, on the other hand, results in a more practical purpose of gaining knowledge from text, which can be used in the world to construct a model, pass a test, conduct an experiment, or understand a phenomenon.

Rarely, however, is any one reading of any one text totally "pure"; that is, totally efferent or totally aesthetic. Rather, as Louise Rosenblatt (1994) reminds us, most readings consist of a blend of both efferent and aesthetic responses, with an emphasis on one or the other depending on the demands of the text and the purpose of the reader. A cookbook, for example, can be read efferently to figure out how to bake a pie, but also present are aesthetic responses to the way the information is presented, the decorative illustrations, or the imagined end product. Or, that same cookbook can become a predominately aesthetic experience, as format and design are appreciated (especially if there are photographs of luscious food), and imagined meals are enjoyed. Both the reader's purpose and the text's inherent possibilities determine how a particular reader reads at a particular time.

Often, what teachers ask students to do determines the stance from which they read, which usually means students read stories and poems from an efferent, and thus inappropriate, stance. Thus historical fiction is read for facts about a time and place, and poetry is read for facts about the poem's construction. The questions that follow selections in a basal reader or that appear in teacher's guides are often oriented toward low-level recall and are essentially tests posed as discussion questions. Many readers learn very early how to find these questions first and then scan the material for the answer. They may never read carefully any selection in their basal readers, no matter how good, because they are looking for those answers that will earn them a good grade. How unfortunate! But how easy to change.

As these second-grade readers read and discussed literature, they needed to be aware of the kind of text being read and how that shaped their purpose for reading. This was encouraged by Lisa through response activities and her comments on the genres they were reading, which was especially salient during the Life Long Ago theme as students read a rich mixture of nonfiction and fiction.

In February, Lisa helps them differentiate what to look for in poetry, fiction, and nonfiction. Chris has just remarked that he does not like the poems about dinosaurs because they make fun of the dinosaurs. Lisa asks if poems can be funny, and he agrees that is all right, but still takes exception to the poems:

> Lisa: Is there a difference between making fun of and having fun with and playing?
>
> Chris: Yes, but this other poem calls dinosaurs "floppy, clumsy idiots" and I don't like that.
>
> Lisa: Okay, so certain poems have a certain tone that you don't like. Why don't the rest of you read these poems and see what you think.

Shida shared a nonfiction book, *The Jurassic Dinosaurs* (by Dougal Dixon), showing the illustrations to the class. Lisa drew their attention to the formatting, telling Shida to look at the box in the illustration to see the length of the dinosaurs. She helped them use the text to obtain information about size. As Shida realized how the book works, he shared his enthusiasm: "On every page it shows how big it is and compares it to people." Lisa concluded by commenting: "That has a lot of good information in it."

Near the end of the discussion Amarachi shares *Professor Curious and the Mystery of the Hiking Dinosaurs* (by Yvonne Gil), a book that mixes a fictional storyline with nonfiction information about dinosaurs and scientific discoveries. After a discussion of solutions to the mysteries that the professor proposes, Lisa comments:

> Lisa: So when I'm thinking about this book and it has dinosaurs with little hiking boots on, it's a...

Group: Fantasy!

Lisa: So when I'm reading this kind of book and I know that it's fantasy, I also know that fantasy often has humor and that in the fantasy some of the solutions might be possible.

Amarachi: (sharing another page) It's not a mountain, it's two continents, and when two continents hit they make a mountain.

Lisa: Is this historical fiction? It seems like it's telling us what scientists found a long time ago and what they knew about how dinosaur footprints got on top of the mountains in Switzerland.

Amarachi shows the group more pictures, commenting on how Asia and Africa came together.

Lisa: It looks like there's a lot of good information in the book, too. You learned a lot of things.

In this conversation, the literature group tried to understand how this particular book worked with its blend of fantasy, historical detail, and scientific information. They would return to this task repeatedly during this theme as they read and discussed other narrative nonfiction books.

Reflection Point

Think about what you ask your students to do when they read a story or a poem. Do you ask them to savor the experience, or do you ask for some fact so you'll know whether they read the selection? Many teachers think that by not asking for factual information students won't read. How do you feel about this? What, if anything, do you do differently when your students are reading a nonfiction text? How do you help them approach different kinds of texts with different stances?

Becoming Engaged Readers

Helping students develop the ability to read from an appropriate stance encourages them to become engaged readers, personally connected with the texts. We want students to be good readers but we also want our students to choose to read, to read for many purposes, and to read in many contexts. Engaged readers "possess beliefs, desires, and interests that energize the hard work of becoming literate" (Guthrie & Anderson, 1999, p. 17). Readers who want to become part of a story world, who are curious, and who want to talk about books with others are engaged, active readers. Lisa structured her reading program to promote engagement. The discussions of this literature group had numerous examples of the results of engaged reading. Below is a brief dialogue that occurred in mid-March, which is emblematic of the kind of emotional engagement with which the students read books. The group is discussing *Skylark*:

> **Jasmyn:** I wanted to share what I think about this chapter. Anna forgot her journal!
>
> **Chris:** I think she's so sad she doesn't want to write. If I were Anna I would be sad.
>
> **Cameron:** I made up a song for page 27. It was a cool song!

The students empathized with the character and were so involved in what was happening to the characters that Cameron had time to make up a song. Repeatedly, these young readers demonstrated their engagement with the stories by their comments during discussion and their passionate arguments about the characters' motivations and feelings.

Reflection Point

Think and write about the following: Is your teaching and curriculum skill driven or comprehension driven? What matters most to you? What messages about reading are sent to your students through the activities you give them?

Teaching Comprehension: Strategies and Skills

As children learn to be literate, they master many different skills such as punctuation or phonics, as they also develop strategies, specific procedures, or ways of doing specific tasks (Jones, Palinscar, Ogle, & Carr, 1987). Strategies are plans that readers apply and adapt to the different texts and tasks they encounter (Pearson, Roehler, Dole, & Duffy, 1992). Good readers employ certain key strategies such as using prior knowledge, asking and answering questions, determining what is important, summarizing, making inferences, dealing with graphic information, imaging, and self-monitoring (Graves, Watts-Taffe, & Graves, 1999). Lisa's demonstrations, direct instruction, questions, and gentle nudgings provided multiple opportunities for learning, applying, and refining effective strategies.

Fluent readers know a variety of strategies and how and when to use them. They can monitor their own learning, realize when they are having trouble, and think about what they can do to help themselves. Strategic learners who are reading new texts make predictions, monitor the accuracy of those predictions, and think about what they are reading until they are satisfied that they understand the text. If they are confused, they might reread, talk to others, or continue to think about what they are reading. Lisa's students learned to do these things through the questions she asked and the directions she gave during literature group discussions. This instruction was repeated throughout the year, as in this discussion of *Bunnicula* in January, when Cameron expresses some confusion:

Cameron:	How would Harold trip over a piece of garlic?
Lisa:	What page are you talking about? Where does it say that he tripped over a piece of garlic?

Sarah offers to show her, but Lisa says no, "I want Cameron to find it." When he does, she asks, "Where was the garlic?"

Cameron:	Lying in the doorway. No, maybe one was upstairs.
Lisa:	Let's go back to pages 62 and 63. "The odor grows stronger as I approached the living room." So who's coming? They're in the same room?
Will:	So Chester was walking in front of Harold, so Harold might have tripped on the piece that Harold was wearing.
Sarah:	No, he tripped on the piece on the floor.

How Harold tripped was not important to comprehending the story, but Cameron, an active reader who created images as he read, was trying to visualize the scene, so it was important to him. Recognizing this, Lisa taught him and the others the valuable strategy of returning to the text, visualizing what was happening through close attention to what the text tells readers, and then making informed decisions. Later in that discussion, as well as in many others, Lisa reminded them to "go back to the text."

Teaching to Learn: Using Pictures to Understand Story

As seen in Chapter 3, the students enjoyed illustrations in the stories and often used them to understand what was happening as well as to enjoy the way in which some illustrations enrich and extend the text. Especially in the early part of the year, Lisa encouraged them to use the illustrations to check their developing comprehension.

In the early September discussion in which Chris shares *Willy and Hugh*, he used the illustrations rather than the text to support his contention that the book is "sad," remarking about the expression on Willy's face, "If that isn't sad I don't know what is." Lisa supported his interpretation, remarking that we get lots of information from pictures in picture books. In the December discussion of *Abuela*, Lisa helped the students look closely at the illustrations to understand that this story was, because of the pictures, fantasy. A focus on illustrations was present right from the beginning. However, as the year progressed, students began to read chapter books rather than picture books, and things began to change.

Remember Sarah's lament that she found it difficult to read chapter books instead of picture books because there were no pictures? Many others, including Pilar, felt this way. But as they read and discussed what they thought and what they saw, they began to rely on their own visualizing rather than that of an illustrator. In March, Pilar comments on this:

> Pilar: From Chapters 12 to 14, I have just discovered that there are no pictures, in Patricia MacLachlan's books, in the chapter books.

Group:	There were in *Arthur, for the Very First Time.*
Pilar:	Not many though, and I wonder why she didn't put pictures in.
Lisa:	What's interesting is why you didn't miss them!
Pilar:	Because I pictured so much that it seemed like they were in here.

Lisa's instruction began with a focus on the illustrations as important to the creation of meaning and ended with a focus on the details in a text that enabled students to visualize as they read.

Teaching to Learn: Compare and Contrast

Early in the year Lisa introduced Venn diagrams as a tool to help her students compare one book to another or one character to another. This strategy encouraged them to focus on both similarities and differences.

It's mid-September, and the literature group is gathered in its usual circle, ready to begin.

Lisa:	Today we are going to talk about using a Venn diagram. Yesterday we talked about the similarities between Little Nino's and Big Nino's. We're going to use two circles. (She explains how to draw the circles and what to put in each section, emphasizing comparing and contrasting, and demonstrating how to construct the diagram.) This is a way to organize. We did this some yesterday. Recall our discussion yesterday? What were some of the differences? How is Little Nino's different from Big Nino's?
Chris:	It serves big pizza.
Cameron:	Big Nino's should be called Little Nino's and vice versa.
Maria:	Little Nino's was small.

Lisa charts the students' responses.

Cameron:	Big Nino's had a huge space.

Shida referred to his book, looking for details and, when Lisa praised him for doing this, Cameron and Amarachi got up to get their books as Chris reached for his. They continued the discussion, elaborating on the differences, until they ended up talking about how money did not make Nino happy. Lisa ended with a review of how to construct a Venn diagram.

Students continued to use Venn diagrams to compare books or characters within books. Sometimes they incorporated the strategy into their journal writing, as Chris did in several of his responses to *The Celery Stalks at Midnight* (see Figure 2).

Figure 2
Chris's Venn Diagram

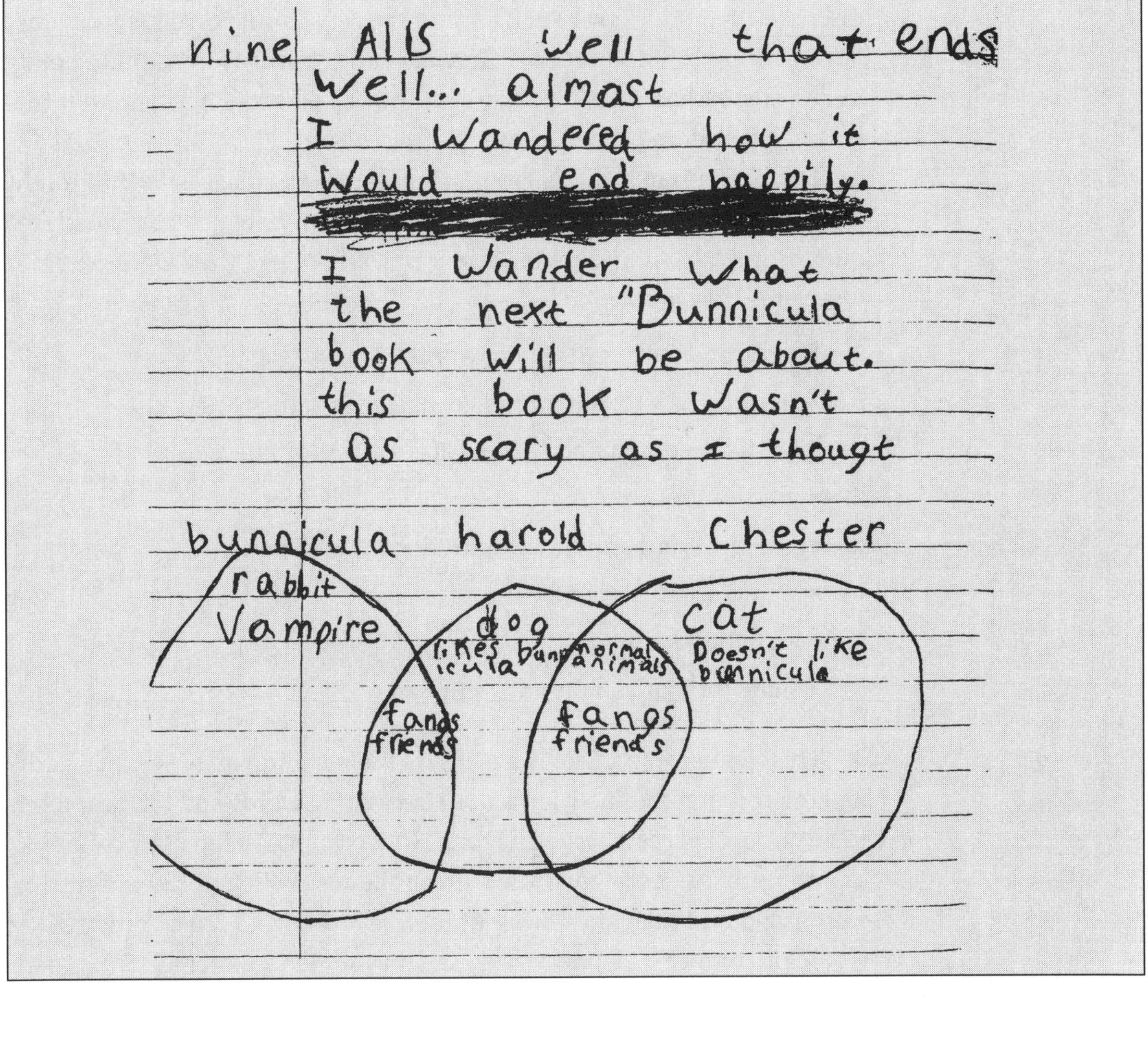

nine Alls well that ends well... almost
I wandered how it would end happily.

I wander what the next "Bunnicula book will be about. this book wasn't as scary as I thougt

bunnicula   harold   Chester

rabbit
Vampire   dog   cat
                 likes bunn normal   Doesn't like
                 icula animals   bunnicula
          fangs   fangs
          friends   friends

At the Word Level: Decoding and Comprehension

Most members of Lisa's literature group were skilled at decoding. Only two students gave an indication of struggling with how to say a word, but many students did not know the meanings of the words they could decode. Lisa worked with the two students who needed decoding instruction during independent reading, taught phonics through her spelling lessons, and focused on strategies for discovering word meaning.

The phonics instruction that the fluent readers received came through their work with weekly spelling words. As Lisa presented the words, they discussed them in terms such as short vowels, long vowels, synonyms/ antonyms, and homophones. They also added words from trade books they were reading to the weekly spelling lists, discussing them in terms of spelling patterns.

More important for this group were the word-attack skills they might employ when they did come to an unknown word, which happened frequently because of the wide variety of trade books they were reading. Over time they learned to

- look for small words in big words,
- see if an unknown word looks like a word they knew,
- see if they could find chunks of a word they knew,
- use the context,
- skip the word and move on (to look it up later),
- sound out the word,
- ask a buddy, and
- share their uncertainty with the group.

This was accompanied by a focus on the meaning of these new words, and the children routinely looked up interesting words and brought them to the group. Lisa established a Word Wonderment Wall to draw children's attention to interesting words. During the week they noted interesting words, and on Friday they brought their favorite word to the group. They would pronounce it, define it, and use it in a sentence. After all had shared, the group voted on a favorite one or two words to add to the Word Wonderment Wall. This was also a way into a discussion of the author's style.

Preparing to Read

Lisa had many ways of preparing the group to read a selection. Because instruction was thematically organized through the basal, she always related new texts to the current theme, either by telling the children how it was related or by asking how it might be related as they read it. Sometimes she might read aloud another book, which served as an introduction to the text they were about to read. At other times she might share relevant information about the author and illustrator or remind students of other texts they had read by the same author or illustrator. When appropriate, she linked a new text to the genres the students had been discussing.

She also prepared students to read a new selection through strategy instruction, such as a picture walk, where they previewed the story through the illustrations. Then they were asked to write a prediction about what the book would be about, share relevant prior knowledge through group discussion, and write in their journals about the topics and ideas they would be reading about. Lisa selected from these strategies according to her students' needs and the demands of the texts, as when she discussed the differences between fiction and nonfiction. In this, as in the rest of her teaching, she was flexible and responsive.

Reading Aloud

Reading aloud to her students was an important part of Lisa's reading program. The students could and, for the most part, did read to themselves with little difficulty, but Lisa felt that reading aloud was still important. By reading aloud, Lisa gave her students experiences with literature they would not have had. Reading a story aloud meant much more than sharing the words and pictures. Reading aloud meant that the students and Lisa all shared the experience of the story simultaneously, and this experience was presented to the students through text and illustrations as well as Lisa's interpretation of these elements or her artistry as an oral reader (see Box 4-2).

Reading aloud helps young children become readers, and it helps older children become better readers. Just as her students adopted the questions she asked, the response formats she demonstrated, and the journal prompts she provided, they also adopted her fluent, dramatic reading style. Many children do not hear fluent, oral reading unless a teacher reads aloud.

Reading aloud extends everyone's horizons: Students gain new experiences and learn new ideas, new vocabulary, and new ways of using words. Reading aloud gave Lisa the opportunity to stop and savor words, thus focusing on style and vocabulary. It allowed her students to hear, not just see, the variations in style that children's literature provides. It allowed her to demonstrate to her students how to build meaning collectively from a shared book experience. It erased many of the differences that existed among her students even though they all could read. Sarah, for example, would have spent all her time struggling to keep up with students who were exceptionally fluent readers. By reading aloud, Lisa allowed Sarah's exceptional oral comprehension to surface, thus giving her a visible strength in the group, which offset her initial weakness in decoding.

Reading aloud was the vehicle through which Lisa introduced her students to longer texts. Their first novel, *Arthur, for the Very First Time*, was presented through oral reading. This kept all the students on the same page in their discussions and helped them to see that they could, indeed, make sense of chapter books after all. It made a daunting task

---

BOX 4-1
Tips for Reading Aloud

1. Read the book ahead of time (if you have time) so that you are familiar with it.
2. Give a brief introduction to the book.
3. Begin reading aloud slowly, then quicken the pace as children begin to attend to the text.
4. Look up from the book frequently to maintain eye contact with your audience.
5. Use your voice and your body to enhance meaning.
6. Stop and comment on interesting ideas, words, descriptions, and if you wish, invite comments from the children.

more manageable. It was also something that Lisa and her students enjoyed tremendously.

Basing her reading program on children's literature was not a simple task. Good teaching is demanding and complex, Lisa was constantly alert for signs of confusion and of growth in her students. Lisa's alertness was rewarded as her students demonstrated an average gain of 4.5 years on their Informal Reading Inventory scores, and scored between the 76th and 99th percentile on the Iowa Test of Basic Skills reading comprehension subtest (see Chapter 5). Although gratifying, the scores were one small manifestation of what the students really learned: to select books, to read with gusto, to actively monitor their meaning-making, and to value the experience of talking about books with others. In short, they learned to be readers.

Reflection Point

Think about your daily teaching routines. How often do you read aloud? Why do you read aloud? Is reading aloud an integral part of your instructional strategy or merely a pleasant time-filler? Write about how you might want to alter your read-aloud program; choose one idea and implement it.

Chapter 5

How Can I Know What My Students Have Learned?

It is late spring, and fuchsia, impatiens, and chirping birds welcome Shane's entrance to the school. As he approaches the classroom, he hears familiar voices—the voices of Lisa's students engaged in discussion of individual books. It's a sound of energy and excitement. He thinks about his own teaching, recognizing the paradoxical delight and dread of spring, which means spring fever and end-of-year testing. Although he, Lisa, and Lee have documented this group's development over time, the informal and formal testing mandated by the school district lurks at the back of their minds, especially Lisa's.

Reading differently in this class meant reading more than words. It meant reading literature deeply and wondering about the meanings of life. And it meant becoming metacognitive readers—reading and thinking about the meaning they were creating. As readers, these students were not uniquely different from other good second-grade readers when they began the school year. But over time and with the help and guidance of a reflective, responsive, and passionate teacher, they learned to read, listen, and think differently.

Lisa set out on a journey of change. She had investigated her own instructional patterns in graduate course work and decided to change her instructional direction. Lisa was an excellent teacher but realized that she could be better. She had tired of the old ways of teaching and wanted her reading instruction to move beyond the static instructional patterns of the past.

As Lisa centered her teaching around a response-based philosophy, she encountered worries and concerns. She was doing something different—allowing students to participate more fully in the educational experience and to have more responsibility for their own learning. She set aside many of the traditional forms of assessment she had used previously. She was asking herself and her students to take more risks.

Teachers and parents were interested in what was happening in Lisa's class. In the beginning of the year, Lisa sent a letter to parents explaining the reading program and her philosophy (see Figure 3 on page 104). She further informed parents through weekly reports, which was the key to parental support. Parents expressed great support for Lisa's innovations and risk taking. Sarah's mother encouraged Lisa, "Sarah is reading more and loves the literature group. Her reading habits have really changed this year." Other parents echoed similar support in conferences. Lisa engaged fellow teachers in discussions of literacy teaching through monthly team meetings. She also presented information about her teaching to other first- through third-grade teachers in her school and later shared her enthusiasm for teaching reading in new ways at a district-sponsored language arts conference. At these meetings, Lisa shared her emergent insights as she engaged in teaching from a new perspective.

Although Lisa was a confident teacher, such broad changes made her anxious in the beginning. Were her new ways working? Would her students perform well on standardized and other required tests? Such questions create an anxiousness typical and expected when teachers make changes in literacy programs, changes that rearrange the purposes and goals of instruction.

Too often in schools, traditional testing and old metaphors of learning have driven the curriculum and the way in which we teach it. In the past, we taught skills, students practiced those skills in isolation, and we in turn tested the skills and then moved on to teach the next set of skills. Our instructional programs were being engineered by a force outside the everyday interactions of students, who happened to be the ones whom we taught.

Figure 3
Letter to Parents

BRAG
Barrow Readers Achieve Goals
David C. Barrow Elementary
Athens, Georgia

Dear Parents,

I am thrilled to have the opportunity to work with your child in a small flexible reading group for 70 minutes each morning. BRAG (Barrow Readers Achieve Goals) time will focus on vocabulary development, guided reading, response to reading, shared reading, and spelling.

Each day students will bring home a plastic BRAG bag containing a book for independent reading, a book log to record books read, a Blue Book Response Journal, and a homework assignment.

Spelling words are assigned on Monday and are integrated with our reading book. Students will have spelling homework Monday - Thursday. Spelling tests are on Friday and tests will be sent home in students' purple folder.

Reading homework will be assigned Monday - Thursday. Students will *usually* be asked to read and write a response. Students should also practice reading aloud (to develop fluency and confidence) the passage they wish to share with the BRAG group the next day.

Finally, I would like to use a portfolio for each student. Portfolios will be sent home and shared with you once each quarter. I have found portfolios help to measure and document the growth of students in second grade. I would appreciate your help by supplying your child with a 3 - ring binder (with a front and back pocket) of at least one and one - half inches.

Please feel free to contact me if you have any questions or concerns. I look forward to meeting you at Barrow's Open House.

Sincerely,

Lisa Cross Stanzi

*Reflection Point*_____

Write a list of your own worries about changing your instructional practice. It is often the fears and worries about change that seem to paralyze any efforts to change. Jot them down quickly and freely. Identify and group them as to what is under your control and what is beyond your ability to change. List the audiences that will be watching your change. Now, write a letter to yourself—of commitment to change—that affirms your fears and worries.

We know a lot about how children learn, and we are beginning to understand how responsive teachers learn from children. We hope it is evident in the preceding chapters that, yes, Lisa's students did learn a great deal as they taught us about their own literacy processes. We know that language is socially constructed and too complex to be simplified in arbitrary ways. Students do need to develop skills and strategies for reading, and they do this best in the process of real reading—reading for many purposes and in many ways. Students also need time to develop, and Lisa not only gave them time, she gave them planned and organized time. Her organization gave students the confidence to take more responsibility for their own literacy learning.

Embarking on a journey of change, Lisa began to envision her teaching in different ways. No longer was she teaching reading to children, she was teaching children to read. And teaching children to read responsively pushed Lisa's instructional program in new directions. Her goals changed. Her conception of literacy teaching shifted, and she began to transform her teaching and learning. She wanted students to know the excitement of understanding life through their encounters with books and understanding books better through their own life experiences. She was crafting a new teaching life for herself, a teaching life that propelled her into asking more questions about instruction and assessment.

Reflection Point_____

Respond to the following questions in your journal:

What are the purposes implicit in the instructional tasks in which students are regularly involved?

What opportunities for social interaction are evident in my language arts program?

Does my classroom provide a variety of situations that promote a diverse range of language use?

How can I shape or reshape instructional practice that will provide greater student involvement and more variety in language use?

As Lisa's goals and purposes for instruction shifted, so did her modes of assessment. Finding ways to study children's academic progress became of paramount importance as Lisa became a reflective, responsive, and planful teacher. Although Lisa already had a passion for teaching, her teaching became more intense and alive as she began looking closely at her teaching and reconceptualizing her notions of assessment.

Lisa began observing children closely as a way of assessing not only the strengths and weaknesses of students but the effectiveness of her changes in teaching and curricula. She became an astute "kidwatcher." Assessment was no longer an end in itself; rather, it became a beginning. It was no longer something you did *to* students but something that you did *with* students. As Lisa adopted and created effective ways of assessment, assessment began to inform her instruction.

Keeping a Journal as Reflective Practice

From the beginning, Lisa kept reflective notes about her teaching. She recorded successes and failures, joys and frustrations, and confidences and insecurities. Keeping a journal became a way for Lisa to validate the day's events or a moment of frustration. From writing-process theory and approaches, we know that writing is a way of thinking and organizing the events of our lives into a reflective record of our processes, a way of claiming our humanness (Calkins, 1994). The following entry describes Lisa's own struggle with interpreting and assessing the day's discussion group:

> 9/10/98 Wednesday
>
> Students shared responses such as "my favorite part" and "I liked the book." We discussed alternative responses. I reminded them to look inside their blue journals. I am still concerned with Cameron and Jasmyn's domination of the discussion. Achala and Amarachi seem very hesitant to talk; in fact they don't unless called upon. I briefly talked to them after class and gave them encouragement to speak up. Will was wound up, and when it was his turn to share he wouldn't speak. I ended up having to take away his BRAG bag [in which books and journals were kept] because it was in his mouth, over his head, etc.
>
> We reviewed cause and effect from Frog and Toad in relation to Henry and Mudge books. The students finished their letters to Toad and we regrouped to share the letters, which were interesting. The best part was when Maria asked, "Why are we writing a letter to Toad? He's not real." So, what an opportunity to talk about entering the world of a story, a great discussion. I am so intrigued by their thinking about reading and what happens when we read. Of course, it would happen at the end of class and we ran out of time. I need to remember to give the group time. I see them growing and trying, and I know that sometimes growth and change is uncomfortable.

Lisa's moments of reflection became forums for thinking about the next day's discussion. Writing in her journal became a vehicle for curriculum planning. Documenting the day-to-day narratives of learning and literature helped Lisa recognize her role in planning instruction (Connelly & Clandinin, 1988). Knowing that learning is not necessarily a linear process affirmed Lisa's practice of moving back and forth between student and instruction. She was shaping her craft day-by-day, searching for the right balance. There was no recipe to follow; indeed, no recipe will do. Instead, we must be open to ongoing, empowering reflection.

In the following journal entry, Lisa recounts the success of a powerful discussion and asks herself important questions: What went well? Who participated in the discussion?

> 9/16/98 Tuesday
>
> Wow! We had a wonderful discussion about *Nino's Pizzeria*. Students were engaged listeners and piggybacked off each other. We were really

able to peel away the layers of the onion! We got right to the nitty gritty of the story. Through the discussion the students realized how important the illustrations are to the text, and we all discovered new things in the illustrations. I am thinking that we need to spend more time in discussion about books that we all read. I believe this is a possible reason why we had such a powerful discussion. The talk is so different when we share books that we all haven't read. In fact, after we finished Nino's discussion, we shared books we read last night and students did okay. However, no one responded to each other. I need to go back and listen to the tape of last Friday when students made connections among the texts. That was another glimpse of the magic they will have in their discussion groups. It is very exciting to see them coming together. Time is still an issue for me. I didn't do all I had planned and, before we knew it, we chose books and off we went.

Many of us want to write in reflection journals, yet we make many excuses. Expectations for ourselves are often too high. We worry about the way we write. We have a misconception that it must come out right the first time, that we need the right notebook, and that if only we had more time, we could do it right. We can crumble our writing block by considering all the ways we have to record and reflect on the data our students provide. The shape of Lisa's journal was eclectic. Her reflective practice was not limited to an 8x10 spiral notebook. Instead, it mirrored the active pace of teaching. She made her entries on whatever was handy: on index cards, in her plan book, and on sticky notes. Again, this process of planned improvisation shows the messiness of change. But Lisa enjoyed the energy of actively noticing children in different ways.

Reflection Point

Take a moment and "read your classroom." Donald Graves, in *A Fresh Look at Writing* (1994), challenges writers to write rapid reflections of their worlds. He calls this "reading the world." Consider some portion of your day and write about it. What did you notice? Who did you notice? How might you explain the day's events? Become acutely aware of the subtleties of life in your classroom and record them.

The Evidence: Using Talk to Assess Student Performance

Although Lisa sensed the overall success of this new mode of instruction, the worries crept in. How might she prove to someone outside the classroom that her students were in fact learning? What evidence could she show? How might her students fare on standardized-assessment measures compared to other students? With the confidence that she was indeed seeing a difference in her students' academic performance, Lisa began collecting artifacts of language use and language learning. It became crucial for Lisa to articulate for others what happened, how it happened, and offer plausible explanations.

Shifts in understanding and defining literacy have challenged teachers to understand, teach, and assess students differently (Langer, 1991). There is renewed interest in personal response, emphasis on the appreciation of social and cultural aspects of literacy, recognition of the interrelated nature of language, and concern for the meaningfulness of materials and tasks (Bisesi, Brenner, McVee, Pearson, & Sarroub, 1998). Lisa began creating alternative means of assessing her students, sharing the responsibility of assessment, and aligning assessment and instruction.

Talking became an important tool for self- and group evaluation. Talking served as a mediator for articulating the processes of reading and responding. Lisa used what she knew about language theory and language learning to provide opportunities for talk about learning. This talk invited students to think about thinking. Talking became a pathway to assessment. Lisa audiotaped and videotaped nearly every session, which was more than mere data collection. It was central to Lisa's assessment processes. She often engaged children in group evaluations of discussion, opportunities for critiquing both verbal and nonverbal behavior. Lisa and her students collectively created standards for discussion and standards for assessing themselves (see Chapter 2). Periodically, Lisa would stop literature discussions to allow students to reflect and respond to the day's events.

Looking at talk was a way to facilitate informal assessment. For example, students might choose to read aloud a favorite story part or return to text to support a comment, while Lisa listened and assessed their fluency, word recognition, and comprehension. These informal assessments were often noted in her journal, or on a notecard or clipboard. (See Chapter 2, which illustrates students learning tasks, procedures of literature discussion, and self-monitoring.)

As shown in preceding chapters, students began to understand how they were contributing to discussions or how they might be constraining possibilities for greater engagement in discussions. Through these reflective discussions and Lisa's think-alouds (see Chapter 4), students became keen curators of learning. Their developing metacognitive ability allowed them to monitor their own learning. As Lisa modeled her own thinking processes, she encouraged students to support their thinking by questioning themselves about conclusions they made about books they were reading.

Reflection Point

Videotape a group discussion. View the tape with students and evaluate the group's processes. Have students jot down what they learn from listening to themselves. What can you learn about your role as teacher? Consider sharing your tape with a colleague. Ask him or her to discuss and interpret the tape with you. By assessing yourself, you can construct an effective program and build confidence in your ability to teach responsively.

Lisa used talking as a way to rehearse reflective practice. She talked with Lee and Shane after a literature-group session, which gave her an opportunity to reflect immediately. She expressed frustrations, asked questions, and posed ideas. Lee and Shane confirmed her hunches, encouraged her efforts, and most importantly, became "critical friends" with whom she could discuss her emerging pedagogical explorations. This opportunity for immediate talk and feedback was unique to her situation and complemented the journal that she kept.

In addition to verbal reflection and group evaluation, the students completed written theme evaluations. The teacher-constructed evaluations asked students to reflect not only on content learning and reading processes but asked them to set goals for future reading (see Figure 4 for an example).

In Figure 4, Brett has established goals for improving both her participation in group discussion and her personal reading practices. There are many other ways that students can record or display their learning (see Box 5-3).

BOX 5-3
Artifacts Available for Assessment

ARTISTIC EXPRESSIONS: Students crafted various art products from murals to sculptures that reflected their aesthetic engagement with text.

INFORMAL READING INVENTORIES: Lisa administered informal reading inventories to students to assess reading growth.

LITERATURE DISCUSSIONS: Using audio and video tapes of class discussions, Lisa and her students regularly revisited literature discussions. Lisa and her students often constructed collective reflections of their ongoing process of learning to talk about literature.

PORTFOLIOS: This was a collection of many artifacts of learning including theme evaluations, art products, reading logs, and writing samples. Students periodically reflected on the items and selected particular items to show their own growth in learning.

READING LOGS: Students recorded the books they had read and the amount of time spent reading. Parents would initial that the children had spent time reading. Lisa gained insight into students' independent reading choices as well as genre preferences.

RESPONSE LOGS: These logs held students' initial responses and showed development over time. The logs were typically a private place for students to record their musings about a story, to record confusing parts, and to try out new forms of response. In addition, students often used these response logs as springboards for discussion.

STUDENT INTERVIEWS/CONFERENCES: Lisa often engaged in informal interviews and conferences with students as they worked individually on readings and assignments. In these brief interactions, Lisa could often gain important information about strategy use and comprehension. Lisa made notes and used them in her evaluation of the students.

Books on alternative assessment

Tierney, R.J., Carter, M.A., & Desai, L.E. (1991). *Portfolio Assessment in the Reading-Writing Classroom*. Norwood, MA: Christopher-Gordon.

Valencia, S.W., Hiebert, E.H., & Afflerbach, P.P.. (Eds.). (1993). *Authentic Reading Assessment Practices and Possibilities*. Newark, DE: International Reading Association.

Barrentine, S.J. (Ed.). (1999). *Reading Assessment: Principles and Practices for Elementary Teachers*. Newark, DE: International Reading Association.

Figure 4
Brett's Theme 4 Evaluation

Brett

Theme 4 LIFE LONG AGO

1. In this theme, which story did you enjoy reading the most?   Why?

I enjoyed reading The Littlest Dinosaurs the most because I learned new things like some dinosaurs were just as big as a cat.

2. What did you learn about life long ago?

I learned some dinosaurs names, how big they were, and when they lived.

3. Which character from this theme would you like to meet?   Why?

I would like to meet Caleb because I think that he would be fun to play with and he is silly.

4. What did you do well in discussion group?

I responded to other people.

5. What would you like to improve on?

I would like to improve on pigybacking on other people.

6. What about your journal?   What are you proud of?

I am praud of writing thoutful questons.

7. What would you like to improve on?

I would like to improve on witing more in my journal.

8. What are your goals for our next theme?

My goal is to read more minutes.

9. How would you like to improve as a reader and a writer?

I would like to improve on writing discriptive words like Patricia MacLaclan.

*Reflection Point*_____

Become a kidwatcher. Observe your students closely. Select one of the assessment strategies that Lisa incorporated in her practice and try it in your own practice. Then analyze the student artifacts. Ask yourself the following questions: What does this artifact tell me about this child? How might I use this information to change my practice? What other artifacts might I use? Create an action plan for the future. Begin slowly. Adopt a few new strategies to add to your current list of assessment tools.

_____

Standards as Benchmarks

Aside from the informal assessments that informed Lisa, there are many ways to formally assess your practice. For example, in 1996, the International Reading Association and the National Council of Teachers of English joined in establishing national standards by publishing the *Standards for the English Language Arts*. Immediately, teachers began thinking about how these standards would affect classroom practice. Although representatives from wide audiences were involved in creating the standards, in order for the standards to have an impact, they must become part of a teacher's life, philosophy, and ongoing classroom practice.

Students are the ultimate beneficiaries of the standards. As Lisa demonstrated, educators can craft meaningful pedagogy that not only meets the list of standards (see Appendix B), but also moves students well beyond. Throughout this book are illustrative examples of how one teacher renewed her practice. Implicit in these examples are the reverberations of the U.S. national standards. However, Lisa's practices are first and foremost constructed with students at the center rather than driven by a set of standards. Although Lisa used the standards to shape her practices, there are other ways she might have done so, just as there are multiple ways that any individual teacher can accomplish the goals and purposes of the standards.

Change in practice occurs over time, which Lisa recognized, and through trial and error her practice developed over time—not overnight. Lisa was a teacher; but more than that, she was reflective, responsive, organized, and knowledgeable. Undoubtedly, Lisa's practices will continue to change because her practices and the standards are both dynamic. As Lisa continues to question in her future practice and pursues her own professional development, she will modify existing models of teaching while providing better literacy learning opportunities for the children in her classroom.

Reflection Point

Review the previous chapters and examples as you read the following connections between the standards and Lisa's practice. Identify examples that show Lisa and her students pursuing literacy while meeting national standards. Consider the list of standards (see Appendix B). Also, view the watch list of the International Reading Association and *Reading Online* at http://www.readingonline.org/electronic/watch for Web sites that link standards and practice. How many of the standards are you meeting? What practices are helping you meet them? What could you improve?

Standards in Practice

In the classroom, Lisa and her students moved beyond the *Standards for the English Language Arts* (1996). We have provided examples that elucidate not only the processes of literacy learning but also the emergence and accomplishment of standards. The following demonstrates how Lisa's practice fulfilled selected standards.

> STANDARD 1. Students read a wide range of print and nonprint texts to build an understanding of texts, of themselves, and of cultures of

the United States and the world; to acquire new information; to respond to the needs and demands of society and the workplace; and for personal fulfillment. Among these texts are fiction and nonfiction, classic and contemporary works.

Lisa and her students explored many different types of texts. They read different genres—fantasy fiction, contemporary realistic fiction, historical fiction, folklore, nonfiction, and poetry, in both picture book and novel format.

Students learned to talk about books and connect their lives to texts and texts to their lives. They shared their own interpretations and listened to others in order to clarify collective interpretations. In an interview, Amarachi, after reading *Arthur, for the Very First Time*, said, "When Bernadette had babies, it reminded me of when my mom had a baby. I felt like Arthur. I felt I wouldn't be needed that much." Amarachi and the other students explored sensitive issues and concerns by reading about characters in books and used these reading experiences to think about themselves.

Students engaged in the telling of family stories as they made connections to literature in their discussions. They were given culminating project opportunities to express themselves in other symbolic forms such as art, music, drama, and writing. For example, during the nature theme study, students observed nature and recorded observations by writing and drawing. Their observations were offered in classroom discussions. They also viewed a video of Lisa's whale-watching vacation, extending their discussion of animals to include her experience. Finally, children brought popular culture into the classroom, discussing a movie, television show, or a favorite song to illustrate a point of view or make a connection to text.

> STANDARD 2. Students read a wide range of literature from many periods in many genres to build an understanding of the many dimensions (e.g., philosophical, ethical, aesthetic) of human experience.

Students self-selected books to read daily, and Lisa ensured that as many genres as possible were included in the themed sets of books she made available. Not only were various genres represented, Lisa made sure that diversity in gender, social class, and ethnicity was also present in the books and later incorporated into discussions. These students learned about books, art, and the human experience.

> STANDARD 3. Students apply a wide range of strategies to comprehend, interpret, evaluate, and appreciate texts. They draw on their prior experience, their interactions with other readers and writers, their knowledge of word meaning, and other texts, their word identification strategies, and their understanding of textual features (e.g., sound-letter correspondence, sentence structure, context, graphics).

Students often did their thinking orally. As thought worked its way into speech, Lisa gained valuable instructional information about students' learning. In discussions, we see how they have developed as critical thinkers. Lisa also offered students strategies for understanding a text and the development of a character. She encouraged them to self-monitor, offered fix-up strategies when students were stuck or confused, and showed them how to help each other as they read with partners. Lisa also encouraged a prediction-confirmation style of reading, asking "What might happen next? Were you right?" This helps students remain as engaged as possible while reading; it further reinforces the notion that reading should make sense.

> STANDARD 6. Students apply knowledge of language structure, language convention (e.g., spelling and punctuation), media techniques, figurative language, and genre to create, critique, and discuss print and nonprint texts.

Lisa used students' talk about books and characters to help them understand the language, technique, and style that authors use. Knowing and understanding the craft of authors enabled students to comprehend more fully the actions of characters and events of a story. For example, Cheng often needed the group to help him with unfamiliar language structures or figurative language.

> STANDARD 9. Students develop an understanding of and respect for diversity in language use, patterns, and dialects across cultures, ethnic groups, geographic regions, and social roles.

Through a careful selection of books to supplement the multicultural selections in the Literature Works series (1997), Lisa created opportunities for students to experience the family of stories. Using books as catalysts, these students shared their own diverse experiences and grew to recognize similarities and celebrate differences. They interacted with one another and with books, often recognizing themselves in the characters.

> STANDARD 11. Students participate as knowledgeable, reflective, creative, and critical members of a variety of literacy communities.

Students often read with their families and friends and would use those funds of knowledge to supplement their emergent understandings of a complex world with many interpretive stances. Because the group members came from several different homerooms, the children learned to become flexible communicators, adjusting to change in various environments every day. Some of them attended after-school programs and again were faced with wider communities of learners. Lisa also varied the small groups and pairs they participated in, requiring them to adjust their communicative styles.

> STANDARD 12. Students use spoken, written, and visual language to accomplish their own purposes (e.g., for learning, enjoyment, persuasion, and the exchange of information).

Lisa continues to receive reports from parents that students are still reading and using reading and writing at home and in the community for various purposes. Lisa encouraged students to read during vacation and many of them did, even documenting the titles and times they spent with books. In group discussions, students would often recommend favorite books that they had read previously or at home. What a testimony to the power of literature and the effectiveness of Lisa as a teacher! Students became increasingly adept at asking real questions—questions about life—questions that matter most.

This is just a sampling of the ways in which Lisa and her students met selected reading and language arts standards. Lisa managed to blend direct instruction and sensitivity with individual and group student response. She responded to the teachable moment and created opportunities for students to grow as readers and writers. What Lisa did is perhaps somewhat unique and certainly cannot be repeated in quite the same way—even by her; however, we can learn much about change and how we might enact it in our classrooms by thinking about the year that

Lisa and the children spent together. Each of us as teachers must craft a teaching life that meets students' needs and local and state standards. Most important in planning responsive reading and language arts instruction is to keep the goals and purposes in mind, and to keep children at the center of instructional decisions.

*Reflection Point*_____

Read other portraits of change such as the Literacy Studies Series copublished by the International Reading Association and the National Reading Conference; the National Council of Teachers of English Standards in Practice Series; and Zemelman, Daniels, and Hyde's (1998) *Best Practice: New Standards for Teaching and Learning in America's Schools*. Look back at the list of standards. Identify the practices in your classroom that help meet the goals and purposes set forth by the standards. Consider writing about your practices, and submit your work to a journal such as *The Reading Teacher* or the journal of your state or provincial reading association.

Beyond the Standards: Facing the Test

Collecting evidence within the classroom for assessment was the easy part. Now we have to convince others of the effectiveness of our practice. This is the critical part—the part in which everyone is interested—principals, parents, and community. How do the students measure up? The collected evidence is the *proof* of what occurred throughout the year: what students learned, how they learned it, and whether the teaching practice is effective. Test scores show how students in Lisa's classroom compared to others. In many ways, it's much like a *verdict*.

Lisa knew that she had a good case from the start. She had engaged in reflective, responsive practice. She had been willing to modify her instructional practice as needed, and she continued to involve herself as a learner. As mandated by the local school, Lisa administered the *Ekwall/Shanker Reading Inventory*, (1993), both as a pretest in early September and again as a posttest in May. No student in Lisa's classroom made less than a three-level gain in reading, which was determined by the instructional leveling in the inventory (see Table 1).

What amazing results! As Sarah resoundingly stated in a spring discussion, these are "some kids!" If this evidence is not compelling enough, the students were also given the Iowa Test of Basic Skills in the spring and did exceptionally well. The scores reported as National Percentile Rank for vocabulary range from 70 to 97, while the scores reported as National Percentile Rank for comprehension range from 76 to 99. Combining these scores reveals that these students performed in the range of 78 to 99 according to overall National Percentile Rank for reading. Although these tests did not drive the instruction in Lisa's classroom, they are often the measures cited most by critics. Lisa's students did very well. They were excellent, flexible readers, and they could engage in even

Table 1
Informal Reading Inventory Scores

Student	Pretest September	Posttest May	Gain
Amarachi	5	9	+4
Brett	3	9	+6
Cameron	4	8	+4
Chris	3	9	+6
Jasmyn	4	8.5	+4.5
Maria	4	8	+4
Pilar	3	6	+3
Sarah	2	6	+4
Shida	3	8	+5

This inventory was used to provide data for grouping, to serve as pre- and posttests to measure a child's growth, and to provide teachers with information on the child's developmental and instructional level. Students were given passages to read aloud, then the passage was taken away and students were asked to answer questions about the passage. The following miscues were counted as formal errors: substitution, mispronunciation, word aided, omission, insertion, repetition, and reversal. To calculate, the number of comprehension questions missed was figured into the equation, which resulted in the student's reading level (grade level). Only the oral portion of this inventory was given. The highest possible score is 9.

the obscure reading tasks found in such standardized tests and perform well. For Lisa, this seemed to only reinforce her belief that children will not only meet, but will rise above expectations when they are offered authentic learning opportunities.

Reflecting on the Year

Lisa, her students, and their parents were convinced that this year-long commitment to reading "differently" had indeed changed them. Now, Lisa was confident that this way of teaching produced results. Lisa's students had become more engaged as readers, reading beyond books and gaining insights about life.

Lisa and her students immersed themselves in worlds of literature, which made a difference. Literature is powerful and possesses life-informing and life-transforming possibilities (McGinley & Kamberelis, 1996). Cullinan and Galda propose that through literature, children "can explore their own feelings, shape their own values, and imagine the lives beyond the one they live" (1998, p. 5). Literature enriches our lives, making us consciously aware of the life surrounding us. Living with characters and living through the experience of literature allows readers to live beyond their lives. Literature has the power "to make us more human, to help us learn to empathize with characters, to crawl inside the skins of persons very different from ourselves" (Huck, 1990, p. 4). The children in Lisa's classroom were afforded the opportunity to imagine the possibilities that literature offers to readers. These possibilities became a part of each reader. Through Lisa's instructional decisions and responsive planning, she was able to engage her students and their parents as well. The parents of Lisa's students were grateful that their children had experienced the passions of reading, and they told her so.

This group will be forever linked by the books they read and discussed during this particular year. As a culminating activity for the year, Lisa asked students to reflect on themselves as readers. Lisa posed the following: "Write about yourself as a reader. Have you changed? How?" Without a doubt they had changed. The students themselves recognized the subtle changes reading had made in their lives.

I try to think deeply into a book. (Amarachi)

I have changed by reading more minutes because at the beginning of the school year I only read 15 minutes a night, and now I read 40 minutes a night. (Brett)

I am reading more chapter books. (Cameron)

I have changed. I yoused to read-like-this, now I read flouently. (Chris)

I have changed because usually I do more things in b.r.a.g. than I do at home. (Jasmyn)

Yes. Books have changed me. I have become more imosnail [emotional]. (Maria)

I have changed because I no bigger words from reading more books. (Pilar)

Yes. [I have changed] by reading harder books. (Sarah)

I have changed a lot since I was in first grade. First I can't read chapter books now I can read chapter books. (Shida)

And Lisa changed too. She wrote,

Reflecting back on the year, I learned to trust myself, the literature, and most of all—the students. Putting students at the center of my teaching and giving students the gift of time (recognizing that learning something new requires time for both me and my students) was the key for me, although, I acknowledge that this change was not always comfortable for me. However, the gift of time allowed the students to learn how to discuss and think about the texts they were reading. The daily repetition of the experience of talking about books was vital in their development as critical readers. I was given the opportunity to get to know these fabulous students as human beings, and over time we developed deeper understandings of ourselves and others. Learning steps to a new dance can be awkward and exhausting, but with practice and patience, you, too, can learn to dance in a new way.

During the last week of school, Lee and Shane joined Lisa's reading group at a local coffee house to celebrate students' accomplishments. During the week, students had engaged in reflecting on their lives and the school year as a whole. They were asked to think of what was most significant about second grade. Then, Lisa and the students read Alma Flor Ada's *The Gold Coin*, shared reflective responses, and prepared individual "golden coins." On the last day we would all be together, students sipped flavored seltzer water, while classical music played softly. Lisa asked students to share their "golden coins." Some of the students' insights are shared in the form of the following found poem.

From the "InSights" of these children, we perceive the subtle power of becoming more than an independent reader; we see the potential of students becoming newly sophisticated readers. Perhaps you will consider this portrait of 1 classroom, 12 children and 1 teacher, and create with your own students new pathways for literacy learning. You'll never look back.

Gold Coins

My gold coins are
my great reading,
encouraging people,
standing up for myself!
My illustrations,
my great writing.
My BRAG teacher Ms. Stanzi,
my mother, my father—
a strong loving family,
to feel such great feelings.
All of my great teachers!

My gold coin:
Dr. Galda gave me
the book
I liked very much.
and
Having fun
READING
Wonderful Books
and
all the great drawings.

I read
Great Books.
I share them
with my friends

that have read
the same book
so we
can link our responses,
so we
can have fun
and
learn from
other people's mistakes.

Just being
in my classroom
helps me
with problems in
my life.

All my friends
are gold coins
because
they teach me.

To read,
to read more books.
I have such
Great Teachers
with me.

Theme Bibliographies

Theme 1: My Family, Friends, and Neighbors

Adoff, A. (1994). In both the families. In Dorothy S. and Michael R. Strickland (Eds.), *Families: Poems celebrating the African American experience*. Ill. John Ward. Honesdale, PA: Boyds Mills.

Angelou, M. (1994). *My painted house, my friendly chicken, and me*. New York: Crown.

Baylor, B. (1977). *Guess who my favorite person is*. Ill. Robert A. Parker. New York: Aladdin.

Baylor, B. (1994). *The table where rich people sit*. Ill. Peter Parnall. New York: Scribner's.

Blume, J. (1971). *Freckle juice*. New York: Four Winds.

Brandenberg, F. (1977). *Nice new neighbors*. New York: Scholastic.

Browne, A. (1983). *Willy and Hugh*. New York: Knopf.

Cameron, A. (1981). *The stories Julian tells*. Ill. Ann Strugnell. New York: Pantheon.

Cameron, A. (1983). *Julian's glorious summer*. Ill. Ann Strugnell. New York: Random House.

Cameron, A. (1986). *More stories Julian tells*. Ill. Ann Strugnell. New York: Knopf.

Cameron, A. (1990). *Julian, dream doctor*. Ill. Ann Strugnell. New York: Random House.

Cleary, B. (1954). *Henry and Ribsy*. New York: Morrow.

Crews, D. (1991). *Bigmama's*. New York: Greenwillow.

de Paola, T. (1981). *Now one foot, now the other*. New York: Putnam.

De Regniers, B.S. (1965). *May I bring a friend*? Ill. Beni Montresor. New York; Atheneum.

Greenfield, E. (1978). *Honey, I love and other love poems*. Ill. Floyd Cooper. New York: Scholastic.

Grimes, N. (1994). *Meet Danitra Brown*. Ill. Floyd Cooper. New York: Lothrop.

Hamanaka, S. (1995). *Be-bop-a-do-walk!* New York: Simon & Schuster.

Henkes, K. (1988). *Chester's way*. New York: Greenwillow.

Jones, R.C. (1991). *Matthew and Tilly*. Ill. Beth Peck. New York: Dutton.

Kellogg, S. (1986). *Best friends*. New York: Dial.

Levinson, R. (1986). *I go with my family to grandma's*. Ill. Diane Goode. New York: Dutton.

Lobel, A. (1970). *Frog and Toad are friends*. New York: Harper & Row.

Lobel, A. (1972). *Frog and Toad together*. New York: Harper & Row.

Lobel, A. (1979). *Days with Frog and Toad*. New York: Harper & Row.

Miles, M. (1971). *Annie and the old one*. Ill. Peter Parnall. New York: Little.

Ness, E. (1966). *Sam, Bangs & Moonshine*. New York: Henry Holt.

Polacco, P. (1987). *Meteor!* New York: Putnam.

Polacco, P. (1988). *The keeping quilt*. New York: Simon & Schuster.

Polacco, P. (1990). *Babushka's doll*. New York: Simon & Schuster.

Polacco, P. (1990). *Just plain fancy*. New York: Dell.

Polacco, P. (1990). *Thunder cake*. New York: Philomel.

Polacco, P. (1992). *Mrs. Katz and Tush*. New York: Bantam.

Polacco, P. (1994). *Pink and Say*. New York: Philomel.

Polacco, P. (1995). *My ol' man*. New York: Scholastic.

Rylant, C. (1983). *Miss Maggie*. New York: Dutton.

Rylant, C. (1987). *Henry and Mudge: The first book of their adventures*. Ill. Sucie Stevenson. New York: Bradbury.

Rylant, C. (1987). *Henry and Mudge under the yellow moon: The fourth book of their adventures*. Ill. Sucie Stevenson. New York: Scholastic.

Rylant, C. (1989). *Henry and Mudge get the cold shivers: The seventh book of their adventures*. Ill. Sucie Stevenson. New York: Bradbury.

Rylant, C. (1994). *Henry and Mudge and the careful cousin: The thirteenth book of their adventures*. Ill. Sucie Stevenson. New York: Bradbury.

Rylant, C. (1994). *Mr. Putter and Tabby pour the tea*. Ill. Arthur Howard. San Diego: Harcourt.

Rylant, C. (1994). *Mr. Putter and Tabby walk the dog*. Ill. Arthur Howard. San Diego: Harcourt.

Rylant, C. (1995). *Henry and Mudge and the bedtime thumps: The ninth book of their adventures*. Ill. Sucie Stevenson. New York: Bradbury.

Rylant, C. (1995). *Henry and Mudge and the best day of all: The fourteenth book of their adventure*s. Ill. Sucie Stevenson. New York: Bradbury.

Rylant, C. (1995). *Mr. Putter and Tabby pick the pears*. Ill. Arthur Howard. San Diego: Harcourt Brace.

San Souci, R.D. (1995). *The faithful friend*. Ill. Brian Pinkney. New York: Simon & Schuster.

Say, A. (1993). *Grandfather's journey*. Boston: Houghton Mifflin.

Tusa, T. (1987). *Maebelle's suitcase*. New York: Macmillan.

Theme 2: Nature at Your Door

Arnosky, J. (1992). *Crinkleroot's guide to knowing the birds*. New York: Bradbury.

Arnosky, J. (1997). *Crinkleroot's guide to knowing animal habitats*. New York: Simon & Schuster.

Baker, J. (1987). *Where the forest meets the sea*. New York: Greenwillow.

Baylor, B. (1974). *Everybody needs a rock*. Ill. Peter Parnall. New York: Scribner's.

Baylor, B. (1975). *The desert is theirs*. Ill. Peter Parnall. New York: Scribner's.

Baylor, B. (1976). *Hawk, I'm your brother*. Ill. Peter Parnall. New York: Macmillan.

Baylor, B. (1984). *If you are a hunter of fossils*. Ill. Peter Parnall. New York: Aladdin.

Cherry, L. (1990). *The great kapok tree*. San Diego: Harcourt Brace.

Cowcher, H. (1988). *Rain forest*. New York: Farrar, Strauss & Giroux.

de Paola, T. (1985). *The cloud book*. New York: Holiday House.

Dorros, A. (1990). *Rainforest secrets*. New York: Scholastic.

Dorros, A. (1991). *Animal tracks*. New York: Scholastic.

Dunrea, O. (1989). *Deep down underground*. New York: Macmillan.

George, J.C. (1993). *Dear Rebecca, winter is here*. Ill. Loretta Krupinski. New York: HarperCollins.

Gibbons, G. (1987). *Sun up, sun down*. San Diego: Harcourt Brace.

Gibbons, G. (1989). *Monarch butterfly*. New York: Holiday House.

Gibbons, G. (1991). *The puffins are back!* New York: HarperCollins.

Gibbons, G. (1992). *Sharks*. New York: Holiday House.

Gibbons, G. (1992). *Stargazers*. New York: Holiday House.

Gibbons, G. (1993). *Frogs*. New York: Holiday House.

Gibbons, G. (1993). *Spiders*. New York: Holiday House.

Greenaway, F. (1992). *Pond life*. New York: Dorling Kindersley.

Gross, R.B. (1971). *What do animals eat?* Ill. Marshall Peck. New York: Scholastic.

Heller, R. (1981). *Chickens aren't the only ones*. New York: Grosset & Dunlap.

Heller, R. (1985). *How to hide a butterfly & other insects*. New York: Grosset & Dunlap.

Heller, R. (1992). *How to hide an octopus & other sea creatures*. New York: Putnam.

Heller, R. (1994). *How to hide a polar bear & other mammals*. New York: Price Stern Sloan.

Hiscock, B. (1994). *The big tree*. New York: Simon & Schuster.

Jenkins, P. (1997). *A safe home for manatees*. New York: Harper Trophy.

Johnson, N. (1997). *A field of sunflowers*. New York: Cartwheel.

Kovacs, D. (1987). *A day underwater*. New York: Scholastic.

Lauber, P. (1994). *Be a friend to trees*. New York: HarperCollins.

Lavies, B. (1989). *Tree trunk traffic*. New York: Dutton.

Lavies, B. (1990). *Backyard hunter: The praying mantis*. New York: Dutton.

Livingston, M.C. (1986). *Earth songs*. Ill. Leonard Fisher. New York: Holiday House.

Livingston, M.C. (1986). *Sea songs*. Ill. Leonard Fisher. New York: Holiday House.

Locker, T. (1997). *Water dance*. San Diego: Harcourt Brace.

Maass, R. (1992). *When autumn comes*. New York: Owlet.

Mason, J.B. (1994). *River day*. New York: Macmillan.

Matthews, D. (1989). *Polar bear cubs*. New York: Simon & Schuster.

McNulty, F. (1994). *Dancing with manatees*. New York: Cartwheel.

O'Mara, A. (1996). *Deserts*. Makato, MN: Capstone Press.

Parker, N.W. (1987). *Bugs*. New York: William Morrow.

Patent, D.H. (1994). *Looking at bears*. New York: Holiday House.

Ryder, J. (1982). *The snail's spell*. Ill. Lynne Cherry. New York: Puffin.

Ryder, J. (1989). *Hello, tree!* New York: McClelland & Steward.

Ryder, J. (1989). *Mockingbird morning*. Ill. Dennis Nolan. New York: Four Winds.

Ryder, J. (1996). *Where butterflies grow*. New York: Puffin.

Ryder, J. (1997). *Shark in the sea*. New York: Morrow.

Schoenherr, J. (1996). *Bear*. New York: Penguin Putnam.

Sheldon, D. (1990). *The whales' song*. Ill. Garry Blythe. New York: Dial.

Siebert, D. (1988). *Heartland*. Ill. Wendell Minor. New York: Crowell.

Siebert, D. (1988). *Mojave*. Ill. Wendell Minor. New York: Crowell.

Simon, S. (1989). *Whales*. New York: Crowell.

Simon, S. (1993). *Autumn across America*. New York: Hyperion.

Simon, S. (1995). *Sharks*. New York: HarperCollins.

Wallace, K. (1996). *Imagine you are a crocodile*. Ill. Mike Bostock. New York: Holt.

Yolen, J. (1993). *Welcome to the green house*. Ill. Laura Regan. New York: Putnam.

Yolen, J. (1996). *Welcome to the sea of sand*. Ill. Laura Regan. New York: Philomel.

Theme 3: Stretch Your Imagination

Atwater, R., & Atwater, F. (1986). *Mr. Popper's penguins*. New York: Bantam.

Browne, A. (1983). *Gorilla*. New York: Knopf.

Faulkner, M. (1987). *The amazing voyage of Jackie Grace*. New York: Scholastic.

Gannet, R.S. (1948). *My father's dragon*. New York: Random House.

Holabird, K. (1990). *Alexander and the magic boat*. Ill. Helen Craig. New York: Clarkson Potter.

Howe, D. & Howe, J. (1979). *Bunnicula: A rabbit tale of mystery*. Ill. Alan Daniel. New York: Simon & Schuster.

Howe, J. (1983). *The celery stalks at midnight*. New York: Simon & Schuster.

Kurt, K. (1997). *The five fingers and the moon*. Ill. Aljoscha Blan. New York: North South Books.

Lewis, C.S. (1997). *Lucy steps through the wardrobe*. Ill. Deborah Maze. New York: HarperCollins.

Lyon, G.E. (1991). *The outside inn*. New York: Orchard.

Noble, T.H. (1980). *The day Jimmy's boa ate the wash*. Ill. Steven Kellog. New York: Scholastic.

Peterson, J.L. (1968). *The Littles take a trip*. Ill. Roberta Carter Clark. New York: Apple.

Peterson, J.L. (1972). *The Littles give a party*. Ill. Roberta Carter Clark. New York: Scholastic.

Peterson, J. (1977). *The Littles and the trash tinies*. Ill. Roberta Carter Clark. New York: Scholastic.

Sadler, M. (1994). *Alistair and the alien invasion*. Ill. Roger Bollen. New York: Simon & Schuster.

Small, D. (1985). *Imogene's antlers*. New York: Scholastic.

Smith, D.K. (1990). *Ace, The very important pig*. Ill. Lynette Hemmant. New York: Knopf.

Steig, W. (1976). *The amazing bone*. New York: Farrar, Straus & Giroux.

Steig, W. (1992). *Dr. De Soto goes to Africa*. New York: HarperCollins.

Teague, M. (1994). *Pigsty*. New York: Scholastic.

Van Allsburg, C. (1979). *The garden of Abdul Gasazi*. Boston: Houghton Mifflin.

Van Allsburg, C. (1981). *Jumanji*. Boston: Houghton Mifflin.

Van Allsburg, C. (1982). *Ben's dream*. Boston: Houghton Mifflin.

Van Allsburg, C. (1983). *The wreck of the Zephyr*. Boston: Houghton Mifflin.

Van Allsburg, C. (1984). *The mysteries of Harris Burdick*. Boston: Houghton Mifflin.

Van Allsburg, C. (1986). *The stranger*. Boston: Houghton Mifflin.

Van Allsburg, C. (1987). *The alphabet theater proudly presents the Z was Zapped: A play in twenty-six acts*. Boston: Houghton Mifflin.

Van Allsburg, C. (1988). *Two bad ants*. Boston: Houghton Mifflin.

Van Allsburg, C. (1990). *Just a dream*. Boston: Houghton Mifflin.

Van Allsburg, C. (1991). *The wretched stone*. Boston: Houghton Mifflin.

Van Allsburg, C. (1992). *The widow's broom*. Boston: Houghton Mifflin.

Van Allsburg, C. (1993). *The sweetest fig*. Boston: Houghton Mifflin.

Van Allsburg, C. (1995). *Bad day at Riverbend*. Boston: Houghton Mifflin.

Westell, K. (1991). *Amanda's book*. Ill. Ruth Ohi. Toronto, ON: Annick Press.

Yolen, J. (1980). *Commander Toad in space*. New York: Coward, McCann & Geoghegan.

Yorinks, A. (1986). *Hey, Al*. Ill. Richard Eglelski. New York: Farrar, Straus & Giroux.

Theme 4: Life Long Ago

Aliki. (1985). *My visit to the dinosaurs*. New York: Thomas Y. Crowell.

Aliki. (1988). *Dinosaur bones*. New York: Thomas Y. Crowell.

Aliki. (1990). *Fossils tell of long ago*. New York: Thomas Y. Crowell.

Arnold, C. & Hewett, R. (1990). *Dinosaurs down under: and other fossils from Australia*. New York: Clarion Books.

Avi. (1994). *The barn*. New York: Avon Books.

Benton, M.J. (1992). *Dinosaur and other prehistoric animal fact finder*. New York: Grisewood & Dempsey.

Branley, F.M. (1989). *What happened to the dinosaurs?* Ill. Marc Simont. New York: Thomas Y. Crowell.

Carrick, C. (1983). *Patrick's dinosaurs*. Ill. Donald Carrick. New York: Clarion Books.

Cole, J. (1983). *Dinosaur story*. Ill. Mort Kunstler. New York: Scholastic.

Cole, J. (1994). *The magic school bus in the time of the dinosaurs*. Ill. Bruce Degen. New York: Scholastic.

Dingus, L. & Norell, M. (1996). *Searching for Velociraptor*. New York: HarperCollins.

Dixon, D. (1987). *The first dinosaurs*. Ill. Jane Burton. Milwaukee, WI: Gareth Stevens.

Dixon, D. (1987). *Hunting the dinosaurs and other prehistoric animals*. Ill. Jane Burton. Milwaukee, WI: Gareth Stevens.

Dixon, D. (1987). *The Jurassic dinosaurs*. Ill. Jane Burton. Milwaukee, WI: Gareth Stevens.

Dixon, D. (1987). *The last dinosaurs*. Ill. Jane Burton. Milwaukee, WI: Gareth Stevens.

Dixon, D. (1998). *Dougal Dixon's dinosaurs*. New York: Boyds Mills Press.

Gil, Y. (1991). *Professor Curious and the mystery of the hiking dinosaurs*. Ill. Bonnie Timmons. New York: Clarkson Potter.

Hopkins, L.B. (1987). *Dinosaurs: Poems*. Ill. Murray Tinkleman. New York: Harcourt Brace.

Joyce, W. (1988). *Dinosaur Bob and his adventures with the family Lazardo*. New York: Scholastic.

Keller, C. (1987). *Colossal fossils: Dinosaur riddles*. Ill. Leonard P. Kessler. New York: Simon & Schuster.

Lasky, K. (1990). *Dinosaur dig*. Ill. Christopher G. Knight. New York: Morrow.

Lauber, P. (1992). *Dinosaurs walked here, and other stories fossils tell*. New York: MacMillan.

Lauber, P. (1994). *The news about dinosaurs*. Ill. Douglas Henderson & John Gurche. New York: Simon & Schuster.

Lindsay, W. (1992). *American Museum of Natural History: Barosaurus*. New York: Dorling Kindersley.

Lindsay, W. (1993). *American Museum of Natural History: Corythosaurus*. New York: Dorling Kindersley.

MacLachlan (1994). *All the places to love*. Ill. Mike Wimmer. New York: HarperCollins.

MacLachlan, P. (1983). *Through grandpa's eyes*. New York: HarperTrophy.

MacLachlan, P. (1987). *Sarah, plain and tall*. New York: HarperTrophy.

MacLachlan, P. (1994). *Three names*. Ill. Alexander Pertzoff. New York: Harper.

MacLachlan, P. (1995). *What you know first*. Ill. Barry Moser. New York: HarperCollins.

MacLachlan, P. (1997). *Skylark*. New York: Harper.

May, J. (1965). *They turned to stone*. Ill. Jean Zallinger. New York: Scholastic.

Most, B. (1984). *Whatever happened to the dinosaurs?* New York: Harcourt Brace.

Most, B. (1989). *The littlest dinosaurs*. New York: Harcourt Brace.

Most, B. (1996). *If the dinosaurs came back*. New York: Silver Burdett Ginn.

Mullins, P. (1992). *Dinosaur encore*. New York: HarperCollins.

Murphy, J.L. (1992). *Dinosaur for a day*. Ill. Mark Alan Weatherby. New York: Scholastic.

Nolan, B. (1990). *Dinosaur dream*. New York: MacMillan.

Norman, D. & Milner, A.C. (1989). *Dinosaur* (Eyewitness Books). New York: Knopf.

Parish, P. (1974). *Dinosaur time*. Ill. Arnold Lobel. New York: Scholastic.

Peters, D. (1989). *A gallery of dinosaurs and other early reptiles*. New York: Knopf.

Prelutsky, J. (1988). *Tyrannosaurus was a beast*. Ill. Arnold Lobel. New York: Mulberry.

Pringle, L.P. (1995). *Dinosaurs! Strange and wonderful*. Ill. Carol Heyer. Honesdale, PA: Boyds Mills.

Pulver, R. (1991). *Mrs. Toggle and the dinosaur*. New York: Scholastic.

Riehecky, J. (1988). *Apatosaurus*. Ill. Lydia Halverson. Chicago: Childrens.

Ripley, C. (1991). *Two dozen dinosaurs: A first book of dinosaur facts, mysteries, games, and fun*. Toronto, ON: Greey do Pencier.

Rounds, G. (1996). *Sod houses on the great plains*. New York: Holiday House.

Sattler, H.R. (1990). *The new illustrated dinosaur dictionary*. Ill. Joyce Ann Powzyk. New York: Lothrop, Lee & Shepard.

Schwartz, H. (1993). *How I captured a dinosaur*. Ill. Amy Schwartz. New York: Orchard.

Siebert, D. (1989). *Heartland*. Ill. Wendell Minor. New York: Harper.

Simon, S. (1990). *New questions and answers about dinosaurs*. Ill. Jennifer Dewey. New York: Morrow.

Turner, A.W. (1985). *Dakota dugout*. Ill. Ronald Himler. New York: Aladdin.

Van Leeuwen, J. (1992). *Going west*. Ill. Thomas Allen. New York: Dial.

Whitcombe, B. (1993). *Dinosaurs*. New York: MacMillan.

Whitfield, P. (1991). *Why did the dinosaurs disapperar? Questions about life in the past*. New York: Viking Penguin.

Whitfield, P. (1992). *MacMillan's Children's guide to dinosaurs and other prehistoric animals*. New York: MacMillan.

Wise, W. (1984). *In the time of the dinosaurs*. Ill. Lewis Zacks. New York: Scholastic.

Zallinger, P. (1977). *Dinosaurs*. New York: Random House.

Theme 5: A Gift of Tales

Aardema, V. (1975). *Why mosquitoes buzz in people's ears: A West African tale*. Ill. Leo & Diane Dillon. New York: Dial.

Ada, A.F. (1991). *The gold coin*. Ill. Neil Waldman. New York: Simon & Schuster.

Ada, A.F. (1995). *Mediopollito/Half chicken*. Ill. Kim Howard. New York: Doubleday.

Arnold, K. (1993). *Baba Yaga: A Russian foltktale*. New York: North-South.

Arquette, M.F. (Ill.) (1994). *The children of the morning light: Wampanoag tales* (as told by Manitonquat). New York: Simon & Schuster.

Bang, M. (1976). *Wiley and the hairy man: Adapted from an American folktale*. New York: Macmillan.

Begay, S. (1992). *Ma'ii and cousin Horned Toad: A traditional Navajo story*. New York: Scholastic.

Brett, J. (1994). *Town mouse, country mouse*. New York: Putnam.

Brown, M. (1961). *Once a mouse*. New York: Scribner's.

Cecil, L. (1995). *The frog princess*. New York: Greenwillow.

Chocolate, D.M.N. (1993). *Talk, talk: An Ashanti legend*. Ill. Dave Albers. New York: Troll.

Climo, S. (1989). *The Egyptian Cinderella*. New York: Harper.

Dayrell, E. (1977). *Why the sun and the moon live in the sky: An African folktale*. Boston: Houghton Mifflin.

de Paola, T. (1983). *The legend of the bluebonnet: An old tale of Texas*. New York: Putnam.

de Paola, T. (1988). *The legend of the Indian paintbrush*. New York: Putnam.

Demi. (1990). *The empty pot*. New York: Holt.

Demi. (1990). *The magic boat*. New York: Holt.

Demi. (1994). *The magic tapestry: A Chinese folktale*. New York: Holt.

Demi. (1997). *One grain of rice: A mathematical folktale*. New York: Scholastic.

Fleischman, S. (1986). *The whipping boy*. New York: Greenwillow.

Garland, S. (1993). *Why ducks sleep on one leg*. Ill. Jean and Mou-Sien Tseng. New York: Scholastic.

Goble, P. (1989). *Iktomi and the berries: A Plains Indian story*. New York: Orchard.

Goode, D. (1989). *Diane Goode's book of American folktales and songs*. New York: Dutton.

Haley, G.E. (1970). *A story, a story*. New York: Atheneum.

Haley, G.E. (1988). *Jack and the fire dragon*. New York: Crown.

Heyer, M. (1986). *The weaving of a dream: A Chinese folktale*. New York: Viking/Kestrel.

Hickox, R. (1997). *Zorro and Quwi: Tales of a trickster pig*. Ill. Kim Howard. New York: Doubleday.

Hong, L.T. (1993). *Two of everything: A Chinese folktale*. Ill. A. Whitman. New York: Puffin.

Johnston, T. (1992). *The cowboy and the black-eyed pea*. Ill. Warren Ludwig. New York: Putnam.

Kellogg, S. (1986). *Pecos Bill*. New York: Scholastic.

Kimmel, E.A. (1991). *The greatest of all: A Japanese folktale*. Ill. Giora Carmi. New York: Holiday.

Kimmel, E.A. (1992). *The four gallant sisters*. Ill. Tatyana Yuditskaya. New York: Henry Holt.

Kimmel, E.A. (1993). *Three sacks of truth: A story from France*. Ill. Robert Rayevsky. New York: Holiday.

Kimmel, E.A. (1994). *Anansi and the talking melon*, Ill. Janet Stevens. New York: Holiday.

Lester, J. (1989). *How many spots does a leopard have?: And other tales*. Ill. David Shannon. New York: Scholastic.

Levine, A.A. (1994). *The boy who drew cats: A Japanese folktale*. New York: Putnam.

Ludwig, W. (1991). *Old Noah's elephants: An Israeli folktale*. New York: Putnam.

Martin, R. (1992). *Rough-face girl*. Ill. David Shannon. New York: Putnam.

Martin, R. (1993). *The boy who lived with the seals*. Ill. David Shannon. New York: Putnam.

Martinez, A.C. (1991). *The woman who outshone the sun*. Ill. Symeon Shimin. San Francisco: Children's Book Press.

McDermott, G. (1974). *Arrow to the sun*. New York: Viking.

McDermott, G. (1978). *The stonecutter: A Japanese folktale*. New York: Penguin/Puffin.

McDermott, G. (1992). *Papagayo the mischief maker*. San Diego: Harcourt Brace.

McDermott, G. (1993). *Raven: A trickster tale from the Pacific Northwest*. San Diego: Harcourt Brace.

McKissack, P.C. (1986). *Flossie and the fox*. New York: Dial.

Miller, M. (1989). *The moon dragon*. New York: Dial.

Mollel, T.M. (1990). *The orphan boy: A Maasai story*. New York: Clarion.

Rodanas, K. (1991). *Dragonfly's tale*. New York: Clarion.

Rucki, A. (1992). *Turkey's gift to the people*. New York: Scholastic.

San Souci, R.D. (1990). *The talking eggs: A folktale from the American south*. Ill. Jerry Pinkney. New York: Dial.

San Souci, R.D. (1992). *Sukey and the mermaid*. Ill. Brian Pinkney. New York: Four Winds.

Schwartz, H., & Rush, B. (1992). *The Sabbath lion: A Jewish folktale from Algeria*. Ill. Stephen Feiser. New York: Harper.

Steptoe, J. (1987). *Mufaro's beautiful daughters: An African tale*. New York: Lothrop.

Tan, A. (1992). *The moon lady*. Ill. Gretchen Schields. New York: Macmillan.

Taylor, H.P. (1993). *Coyote places the stars*. New York: Simon & Schuster.

Wahl, J. (1991). *Tailypo!* New York: Holt.

Williams, J. (1976). *Everyone knows what a dragon looks like*. Ill. Mercer Mayer. New York: Four Winds.

Wood, A. (1987). *Heckedy peg*. Ill. Don Wood. San Diego: Harcourt Brace.

Yee, P. (1990). *Tales from gold mountain: Stories of the Chinese in the New World*. New York: Macmillan.

Yep, L. (1993). *The butterfly boy*. Ill. Jeanne M. Lee. New York: Farrar, Strauss & Giroux.

Yep, L. (1993). *The man who tricked a ghost*. Ill. Isadore Seltzer. New York: Troll.

Yolen, J. (1988). *The emperor and the kite*. New York: Putnam.

Young, E. (1989). *Lon po po: A red-riding hood story from China*. New York: Philomel.

Young, E. (1992). *Seven blind mice*. New York: Philomel.

Young, E. (1995). *Cat & Rat: The legend of the Chinese Zodiac*. New York: Philomel.

Young, E. (1995). *Night visitors*. New York: Philomel.

Theme 6: Sharing Our Lives

Ada, A.F. (1993). *My name is Maria Isabel*. New York: Simon & Schuster.

Bradby, M. (1995). *More than anything else*. Ill. Chris Soentpiet. New York: Orchard.

Cherry, L. (1992). *A river ran wild: An environmental history*. New York: Dutton.

Cooney, B. (1988). *Island boy*. New York: Viking, Penguin.

Dawson, M.L. (1993). *Over here it's different: Carolina's story*. New York: Macmillan.

Fenner, C. (1995). *Yolonda's genius*. New York: McEldery/Simon.

Flournoy, V. (1985). *The patchwork quilt*. Ill. Jerry Pinkney. New York: Dial.

Flournoy, V. (1995). *Celie and the harvest fiddler*. New York: Tambourine.

Fox, P. (1997). *A likely place*. New York: Aladdin.

Friedman, I.R. (1987). *How my parents learned to eat*. Ill. Allen Say. New York: Houghton Mifflin.

Garland, S. (1993). *The lotus seed*. San Diego: Harcourt Brace.

Houston, G. (1992). *My great-aunt Arizona*. Ill. Susan Lamb. New York: HarperCollins.

Kroll, V.L. (1992). *Masai and I*. New York: Simon & Schuster.

Kuklin, S. (1992). *How my family lives in America*. New York: Bradbury Press.

Leigh, N.K. (1993). *Learning to swim in Swaziland: A child's eye view of a Southern African country*. New York: Scholastic.

Low, W. (1997). *Chinatown*. New York: Henry Holt and Company.

Medearis, A.S. (1994). *Our people*. New York: Atheneum.

Oberman, S. (1994). *The always prayer shawl*. Ill. Ted Lewin. Honesdale, PA: Boyds Mills Press.

Pinkney, G.J. (1994). *The Sunday outing*. Ill. Jerry Pinkney. New York: Dial.

Polacco, P. (1991). *Appelemando's dreams*. New York: Philomel.

Polacco, P. (1992). *Picnic at mudsock meadow*. New York: Philomel.

Polacco, P. (1996). *Aunt Chip and the great Triple Creek Dam affair*. New York: Philomel.

Rattigan, J.K. (1993). *Dumpling soup*. New York: Little, Brown.

Rylant, C. (1982). *When I was young in the mountains*. Ill. Diane Goode. New York: Dutton.

Rylant, C. (1997). *The blue hill meadows*. Ill. Ellen Beier. New York: Scholastic.

Say, A. (1993). *Grandfather's journey*. Boston: Houghton Mifflin.

Stolz, M. (1989). *Storm in the night*. Ill. Pat Cummings. New York: Harper.

Thomas, J.R. (1981). *The comeback dog*. New York: Bantam Doubleday Dell.

Widman, C.B. (1992). *The lemon drop jar*. New York: Macmillan.

Williams, K.L. (1990). *Galimoto*. New York: Lothrop.

Wong, J.S. (1994). *Good luck gold*. New York: McElderry.

Appendix B

IRA / NCTE Standards for the English Language Arts

The vision guiding these standards is that all students must have the opportunities and resources to develop the language skills they need to pursue life's goals and to participate fully as informed, productive members of society. These standards assume that literacy growth begins before children enter school as they experience and experiment with literacy activities—reading and writing and associating spoken words with their graphic representations. Recognizing this fact, these standards encourage the development of curriculum and instruction and make productive use of the emerging literacy abilities that children bring to school. Furthermore, the standards provide ample room for the innovation and creativity essential to teaching and learning. They are not prescriptions for particular curriculum or instruction.

Although we present these standards as a list, we want to emphasize that they are not distinct and separable; they are in fact, interrelated and should be considered as a whole.

1. Students read a wide range of print and nonprint texts to build an understanding of texts, of themselves, and of cultures of the United States and the world; to acquire new information; to respond to the needs and demands of society and the workplace; and for personal fulfillment. Among these texts are fiction and nonfiction, classic and contemporary works.

2. Students read a wide range of literature from many periods in many genres to build an understanding of the many dimensions (e.g., philosophical, ethical, aesthetic) of human experience.

3. Students apply a wide range of strategies to comprehend, interpret, evaluate, and appreciate texts. They draw on their prior experience, their interactions with other readers and writers, their knowledge of word meaning, and other texts, their word identification strategies, and their understanding of textual features (e.g., sound-letter correspondence, sentence structure, context, graphics).

4. Students adjust their use of spoken, written, and visual language (e.g., conventions, style, vocabulary) to communicate effectively with a variety of audiences and for different purposes.

5. Students employ a wide range of strategies as they write and use different writing process elements appropriately to communicate with different audiences for a variety of purposes.

6. Students apply knowledge of language structure, language convention (e.g., spelling and punctuation), media techniques, figurative language, and genre to create, critique, and discuss print and nonprint texts.

7. Students conduct research on issues and interests by generating ideas and questions, and by posing problems. They gather, evaluate, and synthesize data from a variety of sources (e.g., print and nonprint texts, artifacts, people) to communicate their discoveries in ways that suit their purpose and audience.

8. Students use a variety of technological and informational resources (e.g., libraries, databases, computer networks, video) to gather and synthesize information and to create and communicate knowledge.

9. Students develop an understanding of and respect for diversity in language use, patterns, and dialects across cultures, ethnic groups, geographic regions, and social roles.

10. Students whose first language is not English make use of their first language to develop competency in the English language arts and to develop understanding of content across the curriculum.

11. Students participate as knowledgeable, reflective, creative, and critical members of a variety of literacy communities.

12. Students use spoken, written, and visual language to accomplish their own purposes (e.g., for learning, enjoyment, persuasion, and the exchange of information).

From *Standards for the English Language Arts*. (1996). Newark, DE: International Reading Association; and Urbana, IL: National Council of Teachers of English.

References

Anderson, R., Hiebert, E., Scott, J., & Wilkinson, I. (1985). *Becoming a nation of readers: A report of the Commission on Reading.* Washington, DC: National Institute of Education.

Bakhtin, M.M. (1981). *The dialogic imagination: Four essays by M. M. Bakhtin* (M. Holquist, Ed.; C. Emerson; & M. Holquist, Trans.). Austin, TX: University of Texas Press.

Bakhtin, M.M. (1986). *Speech genres and other late essays* (V.W. McGee, Trans.). Austin, TX: University of Texas Press.

Barrentine, S.J. (Ed.). (1999). *Reading assessment: Principles and practices for elementary teachers.* Newark, DE: International Reading Association.

Beach, R., & Wendler, L. (1987). Developmental differences in response to a story. *Research in the Teaching of English, 21,* 286–297.

Bisesi, T., Brenner, D., McVee, M., Pearson, P.D., & Sarroub, L.K. (1998). Assessment in literature-based reading programs: Have we kept our promises? In T.E. Raphael & K.H. Au (Eds.), *Literature-based instruction: Reshaping the curriculum* (pp. 239–260). Norwood, MA: Christopher-Gordon.

Block, K.C., deLain, M.T., Dewitz, P. A., Englebretson, R., Florio-Ruane, S., Galda, L., Grant, C.A., Hiebert, E., Invernizzi, M., Juel, C., Moll, L.C., Paratore, J.R., Pearson, P.D., Raphael, T.E., & Rueda, R. (1996/1997). *Literature works.* Needham, MA: Silver Burdett Ginn.

Britton, J.N. (1970). *Language and learning.* Portsmouth, NH: Heinemann.

Bruner, J.S. (1986). *Actual minds, possible worlds.* Cambridge, MA: Harvard University Press.

Bruner, J.S. (1990). *Acts of meaning.* Cambridge: Harvard University Press.

Calkins, L.M. (1994). *The art of teaching writing* (2nd ed.). Portsmouth, NH: Heinemann.

Cazden, C.B. (1988). *Classroom discourse: The language of teaching and learning.* Portsmouth, NH: Heinemann.

Connelly, F.M., & Clandinin, D.J. (1988). *Teachers as curriculum planners: Narratives of experience.* New York: Teachers College Press.

Cullinan, B.E., & Galda, L. (1998). *Literature and the child* (4th ed.). New York: Harcourt Brace.

Daniels, H. (1994). *Literature circles: Voice and choice in the student-centered class-room.* York, ME: Stenhouse.

Dillon, D., & Searle, D. (1981). The role of language in one first-grade classroom. *Research in the Teaching of English, 15*(4), 311–328.

Ekwall, E.E., & Shanker, J.L. (1993). *Ekwall/Shanker reading inventory* (3rd ed.). Boston, MA: Allyn & Bacon.

Galda, L. (1988). Readers, texts, and contexts: A response-based view of literature in the classroom. *The New Advocate, 1*(2), 92–102.

Galda, L., Cullinan, B. E., & Strickland, D.S. (1997). *Language, literacy, and the child* (2nd ed.). New York: Harcourt Brace.

Gambrell, L.B., & Almasi, J.F. (Eds.). (1996). *Lively discussions! Fostering engaged reading.* Newark, DE: International Reading Association

Goodman, K.S. (1985). Transactional psycholinguistics model: Unity in reading. In H. Singer & R.B. Ruddell (Eds.), *Theoretical models and processes of reading* (3rd ed., pp. 813–840). Newark, DE: International Reading Association.

Graves, D.H. (1983). *Writing: Teachers and children at work.* Portsmouth, NH: Heinemann.

Graves, D.H. (1994). *A fresh look at writing.* Portsmouth, NH: Heinemann.

Graves, M.F., Watts-Taffe, S.M., & Graves, B.B. (1999). *Essentials of elementary reading* (2nd ed.). Needham Heights, MA: Allyn & Bacon.

Guthrie, J.T., & Anderson, E. (1999). Engagement in reading: Processes of motivated, strategic, knowledgeable, social readers. In J.T. Guthrie & D.E. Alvermann (Eds.), *Engaged reading: Processes, practices, and policy implications* (pp. 17–45). New York: Teachers College Press.

Huck, C. (1990). The power of children's literature in the classroom. In K.G. Short & K.M. Pierce (Eds.), *Talking about books: Creating literate communities* (pp. 3–16). Portsmouth, NH: Heinemann.

International Reading Association and National Council of Teachers of English. (1996). *Standards for the English language arts.* Newark, DE, & Urbana, IL: Authors.

Jones, B.F., Palincsar, A.S., Ogle, D.S., & Carr, E.G. (Eds.). (1987). *Strategic teaching and learning: Cognitive instruction in the content areas.* Alexandria, VA: Association of Supervision and Curriculum Development.

Hirsch, K. (1997). I can't be like Pippi 'cause I'm afraid to live alone. In N.J. Karolides (Ed.), *Reader response in elementary classrooms: Quest and discovery.* Mahweh, NJ: Erlbaum.

Kiefer, B.Z. (1994). *The potential of picturebooks: From visual literacy to aesthetic understanding.* New York: Prentice Hall.

Kiefer, B.Z. (1999). *Wings of an artist: Children's book illustrators talk about their art.* New York: Harry N. Abrams.

Langer, J. A. (1991) *Literacy understanding and literature instruction* (Tech. Report No. 2.11). University at Albany, NY: Center for the Learning and Teaching of Literature.

Langer, J.A. (1995). *Envisioning literature: Literary understanding and literature instruction.* New York: Teachers College Press.

Many, J., & Cox, C. (Eds.). (1992). *Reader stance and literary understanding: Exploring the theories, research, and practice*. Norwood, NJ: Ablex.

McGinley, W., & Kamberelis, G. (1996). *Maniac Magee* and *Ragtime Tumpie*: Children negotiating self and world through reading and writing. *Research in the Teaching of English, 30*(1), 75–113.

McMahon, S.I. (1997). Book clubs: Contexts for students to lead their own discussions. In S.I. McMahon, T.E. Raphael, V.J. Goatley, & L.S. Pardo (Eds.), *The book club connection: Literacy learning and classroom talk* (pp. 89–106). Newark, DE, & New York: International Reading Association & Teachers College Press.

Mehan, H. (1979). *Learning lessons: Social organization in the classroom*. Cambridge, MA: Harvard University Press.

Newkirk, T., & McClure, P. (1992). *Listening in: Children talk about books (and other things)*. Portsmouth, NH: Heinemann.

Nodelman, P. (1990). *Words about pictures: The narrative art of children's picture books*. Athens, GA: University of Georgia Press.

Pearson, P.D., Roehler, L.R., Dole, J.A., & Duffy, G.G. (1992). Developing expertise in reading comprehension. In S.J. Samuels & A.E. Farstrup (Eds.), *What research has to say about reading instruction* (2nd ed., pp. 145–199). Newark, DE: International Reading Association.

Rosenblatt, L.M. (1994). *The reader, the text, the poem: The transactional theory of the literary work*. Carbondale, IL: Southern Illinois University Press. (Original work published in 1978)

Rosenblatt, L.M. (1995). *Literature as exploration*. New York: The Modern Language Association. (Original work published in 1938)

Samway, K.D., & Whang, G. (1996). *Literature study circles in a multicultural classroom*. York, ME: Stenhouse.

Shannon, P., Kameenui, E., & Baumann, J. (1988). An investigation of children's ability to comprehend character motives. *American Educational Research Journal, 25*(3), 441–462.

Short, K.G., & Pierce, K.M. (1998). *Talking about books: Literature discussion groups in K–8 classrooms*. Portsmouth, NH: Heinemann.

Sipe, L.R. (1998). How picture books work: A semiotically framed theory of text-picture relationships. *Children's Literature in Education, 29*(2), 97–108.

Sipe, L.R. (1998). Individual literary response styles of young children. *National Reading Conference Yearbook, 47*, 76–89.

Tierney, R. J., Carter, M.A., & Desai, L.E. (1991). *Portfolio assessment in the reading-writing classroom*. Norwood, MA: Christopher-Gordon.

Valencia, S.W., Hiebert, E.H., & Afflerbach, P.P. (Eds.). (1993). *Authentic reading assessment: Practices and possibilities*. Newark, DE: International Reading Association.

Vygotsky, L.S. (1978). *Mind in society: The development of higher psychological processes*. Cambridge, MA: Harvard University Press.

Vygotsky, L.S. (1986). *Thought and language* (A. Kozulin, Trans.). Cambridge: MIT Press. (Original work published 1934)

Wilhelm, J.D. (1995). *"You gotta be the book": Teaching engaged and reflective reading with adolescents*. New York & Urbana, IL: Teachers College Press & National Council of Teachers of English.

Zemelman, S., Daniels, H., & Hyde, A. (1998). *Best practice: New standards for teaching and learning in America's schools* (2nd ed.). Portsmouth, NH: Heinemann.

Children's Book References

Ada, A.F. (1991). *The gold coin*. New York: Atheneum.

Angelou, M. (1994). *My painted house, my friendly chicken, and me*. Photographer, Margaret Courney-Clark. New York: Crown.

Barbour, K. (1990). *Little Nino's pizzeria*. New York: Harcourt Brace.

Baylor, B. (1994). *The table where rich people sit*. Ill. Peter Parnall. New York: Atheneum.

Browne, A. (1985). *Gorilla*. New York: Knopf.

Browne, A. (1991). *Willy and Hugh*. New York: Random House

Crews, D. (1991). *Bigmama's*. New York: Greenwillow.

De Regniers, B.S. (1971). *May I bring a friend*? Ill. Beni Montresor. New York: Atheneum.

Dixon, D. (1987). *The Jurassic dinosaurs*. Ill. Jane Burton. Milwaukee, WI: Gareth Stevens.

Dorros, A. (1991). *Abuela*. Ill. Elisa Kleven. New York: Dutton.

Fleischman, P. (1991). *Time train*. Ill. Claire Ewart. New York: HarperCollins.

Fleischman, S. (1986). *The whipping boy*. New York: Greenwillow.

Gil, Y. (1991). *Professor Curious and the mystery of the hiking dinosaurs*. Ill. Bonnie Timmons. New York: Clarkson Potter.

Gonzalez, L.M. (1994). *The bossy gallito*. Ill. Lulu Delacre. New York: Scholastic.

Henkes, K. (1988). *Chester's way*. New York: William Morrow.

Henkes, K. (1990). *Julius, the baby of the world*. New York: Greenwillow.

Howe, J. (1983). *The celery stalks at midnight*. New York: Simon & Schuster.

James, S. (1991). *Dear Mr. Blueberry*. New York: McElderry.

Jones, R.C. (1995). *Matthew and Tilly*. Ill. Beth Peek. New York: Puffin.

Kellogg, S. (1993). *The mysterious tadpole*. New York: Dial.

Le Guin, U.K. (1990). *Catwings*. Ill. Steven Schlinder. New York: Scholastic.

Lobel, A. (1987). *Frog and Toad are friends*. New York: HarperCollins.

MacLachlan, P. (1985). *Sarah, plain and tall*. New York: HarperCollins.

MacLachlan, P. (1987). *Arthur, for the very first time*. New York: HarperCollins.

MacLachlan, P. (1994). *All the places to love*. Ill. Mike Wimmer. New York: HarperCollins.

MacLachlan, P. (1994). *Skylark*. New York: HarperCollins.

MacLachlan, P. (1995). *What you know first*. Ill. Barry Moser. New York: Harper-Collins.

Medearis, A.S. (1995). *The adventures of Sugar and Junior*. Ill. Nancy Poydar. New York: Holiday House.

Mora, P. (1992). *A birthday basket for Tia*. Ill. Cecily Lang. New York: Simon & Schuster.

Most, B. (1989). *The littlest dinosaurs*. SanDiego: Harcourt Brace.

Ness, E. (1971). *Sam, Bangs, and Moonshine*. New York: Henry Holt.

Polacco, P. (1994). *Pink and Say*. New York: Philomel.

Rylant, C. (1988). *All I see*. Ill. Peter Catalanotto. New York: Orchard.

Rylant, C. (1989). *Henry and Mudge get the cold shivers: The seventh book of their adventures*. Ill. Sucie Stevenson. New York: Bradbury.

Rylant, C. (1994). *Henry and Mudge and the careful cousin: The thirteenth book of their adventures*. Ill. Sucie Stevenson. New York: Bradbury.

Rylant, C. (1994). *Mr. Putter and Tabby pour the tea*. Ill. Arthur Howard. SanDiego: Harcourt Brace.

San Souci, R.D. (1995). *The faithful friend*. Ill. Brian Pinkney. New York: Simon & Schuster.

Say, A. (1993). *Grandfather's journey*. New York: Houghton Mifflin.

Sendak, M. (1963). *Where the wild things are*. New York: Harper.

Schwartz, A. (1984). *In a dark, dark room*. Ill. Dirk Zimmer. New York: Harper-Collins.

Taylor, H.P. (1993). *Coyote places the stars*. New York: Simon & Schuster.

Teague, M. (1994). *Pigsty*. New York: Scholastic.

Van Allsburg, C. (1982). *Ben's dream*. Boston: Houghton Mifflin.

Van Allsburg, C. (1983). *The wreck of the Zephyr*. Boston: Houghton Mifflin.

Van Allsburg, C. (1986). *The stranger*. Boston: Houghton Mifflin.

Van Allsburg, C. (1987). *The Z was zapped*. Boston: Houghton Mifflin.

Van Allsburg, C. (1993). *The sweetest fig*. Boston: Houghton Mifflin.

Author Index

Subject Index